Learning Zurb Foundation

Construct cross-platform and responsive
web pages with the most advanced mobile-first
frontend framework available

Kevin Horek

BIRMINGHAM - MUMBAI

Learning Zurb Foundation

First published: August 2014

Production reference: 1140814

Published by Packt Publishing Ltd.
Livery Place
35 Livery Street
Birmingham B3 2PB, UK.

ISBN 978-1-78216-426-5

www.packtpub.com

Cover image by Artie Ng (artherng@yahoo.com.au)

Credits

Author

Kevin Horek

Reviewers

Olusegun Adegboyega - Edun

Bass Jobsen

Andrea Moretti

Augusto Tijerina

Acquisition Editor

Owen Roberts

Content Development Editor

Arun Nadar

Technical Editors

Veena Pagare

Anand Singh

Copy Editors

Deepa Nambiar

Karuna Narayanan

Laxmi Subramanian

Project Coordinator

Priyanka Goel

Proofreaders

Simran Bhogal

Ameesha Green

Indexers

Mariammal Chettiyar

Tejal Soni

Graphics

Abhinash Sahu

Production Coordinator

Manu Joseph

Cover Work

Manu Joseph

About the Author

Kevin Horek was born and raised in Edmonton, Alberta, Canada, and still lives there with his wife and dog. He will soon be a dad. He works as a senior UX designer / frontend developer. He graduated from NAIT's multimedia program with honors and also from University of Alberta's web builder program with honors and spent a summer studying corporate design at UCLA. He has been designing websites and developing the frontend for over 14 years. He has worked on websites, web apps, and mobile apps. He remembers the days when people used to use tables for layout. He has worked on projects for BMW, Best Buy, Qantas Airlines, Emirates Airlines, CB Richard Ellis, Grubb & Ellis, Cushman & Wakefield, and Colliers International. His work has won site of the day, best site of the year for Colliers International, and has been published in Hit Parader magazine.

About the Reviewers

Olusegun Adegboyega - Edun (whose really long and cool Yoruba name means God is victorious) is a graduate from the Yaba College of Technology with a degree in fine arts. He began his career in graphic design as an art director for some of the world's leading advertising agencies such as TBWA/Concept, SO&U Saatchi and Saatchi, and Lagos. His life was simple back then. All he had to do was work with his creative team to cook up powerful and disruptive advertising ideas, execute those ideas with pixel-perfect art direction in print and/or TV, and basically call it a day.

But then something happened. He was bitten by the interactive media design bug. He fell in love with Flash and 3D animation. However, with few opportunities for this budding new field in Nigeria, he moved to the United States; learned some HTML, CSS, and Flash; and promptly began to freelance as a web designer. He later went back to school and bagged a Bachelor's degree in Graphic Design at Shippensburg University, Pennsylvania. While in college, he created an augmented reality art installation and took an internship at Highrock Studios, a web development company based in Hagerstown, MD. Here, he was introduced to the dark art of responsive web design with Zurb Foundation 3 and Drupal CMS.

With superior right brain skills (creativity, empathy, and so on) and spock-like left brain functions (logic, order, and so on), he knew what he wanted to do when he grew up: become a frontend web developer with a passion for story-driven web design. After graduating from college, he took up some freelance jobs before landing at a frontend web development gig at 717 Studios, a nurturing and caring environment, where two great Jedi masters, Emily Bear (one of the best user interface designers in Pennsylvania) and Chris Mowers (the yoda of application development) took him under their wings and taught him lots of cool web Jedi tricks so that someday he may rule the world of web design and development without crossing over to the dark side of factory-processed, story-less web design.

He continues to be passionate about story-driven design and responsive design with Zurb Foundation. He believes that with the web technologies available now, what you can build is only limited by your own imagination, and therefore, stories and engaging web content are the future of Web 3.0.

He is currently working on a CG illustrated book with augmented reality components woven into it. You can find out more about him and his projects at www.victoredun.com.

I would like to acknowledge my amazing team at 717 Studios (www.717studios.com) for their support. I would like to thank my beautiful wife, Thelma Adegboyega - Edun, for supporting my quest for web development mastery through her encouragement and prayers. I would also like to thank my son, John Edun, who helped me set my priorities as his dad first and web developer second by making sure I have time to read a book to him or even catch cartoon shows such as Regular Show, Spongebob Squarepants, and Adventure Time with him.

Bass Jobsen is from the Netherlands. He has been programming the Web since 1995. From C to PHP, he has always been looking for the most accessible interfaces. He has special interests for the process between designing and programming. In his opinion, web interfaces should work independent of the device or browser.

He is also the author of *Less Web Development Essentials, Packt Publishing*, and at the moment is writing *Less Web Development Cookbook, Packt Publishing*.

Currently, he writes a blog (http://bassjobsen.weblogs.fm/), writes LBS programs for mobile devices (http://www.gizzing.nl), and deploys awesome websites such as http://www.streetart.nl/ and http://www.argfutbol.net/.

He is always happy to help you at http://stackoverflow.com/users/1596547/bass-jobsen. You can also check his WordPress Bootstrap Starter Theme (JBST) and other projects at GitHub (https://github.com/bassjobsen).

Andrea Moretti was born in 1987 in Rome where he currently lives. He dreamed of becoming a scientist in his childhood. He was first introduced to programming languages at 11 when he casually found QBASIC on an old 486 laptop. He is studying Computer Science at Università La Sapienza in Rome, but is proudly a bad student. He strongly believes that working with inspiring people and being passionate about new things is way more effective than exams.

He also spent one year studying about Erasmus at Universidad de Las Palmas de Gran Canaria. This did not help with exams, but being able to live and work in a multicultural environment is invaluable in his humble opinion. He is currently collaborating with Eikona Photography and Digital Imaging as a photographer, IT specialist, and web designer.

As a web designer, he has created various websites for individuals and small companies, mainly using static site generators or WordPress custom themes, often with the help of frameworks such as Zurb Foundation. He is also an active member of RomaJS user group.

He has contributed to various open source projects such as developing and maintaining various skeletons to use Foundation on different static site generators. To know more about him, visit `https://github.com/axyz`.

> I'd like to thank the entire GitHub community for helping me expand my knowledge as a developer and all the open source world for demonstrating every day that sharing and cooperating works better than closing and competing.

Augusto Tijerina is a project manager and web developer who specializes in open source technologies and business solutions. He has worked at WSI for 3 years providing web-based solutions to many clients. He also has a start-up Nuvems.com.

He also reviewed the book *Instant Zurb Foundation 4, Jorge Arévalo and Carlos Azaustre, Packt Publishing*.

> I'd like to thank the staff at Packt Publishing for their professionalism and the author for his great work on this book. On a personal note, I thank Astryd for her continuous love and support.

www.PacktPub.com

Support files, eBooks, discount offers, and more

You might want to visit www.PacktPub.com for support files and downloads related to your book.

Did you know that Packt offers eBook versions of every book published, with PDF and ePub files available? You can upgrade to the eBook version at www.PacktPub.com and as a print book customer, you are entitled to a discount on the eBook copy. Get in touch with us at service@packtpub.com for more details.

At www.PacktPub.com, you can also read a collection of free technical articles, sign up for a range of free newsletters and receive exclusive discounts and offers on Packt books and eBooks.

http://PacktLib.PacktPub.com

Do you need instant solutions to your IT questions? PacktLib is Packt's online digital book library. Here, you can access, read and search across Packt's entire library of books.

Why subscribe?

- Fully searchable across every book published by Packt
- Copy and paste, print and bookmark content
- On demand and accessible via web browser

Free access for Packt account holders

If you have an account with Packt at www.PacktPub.com, you can use this to access PacktLib today and view nine entirely free books. Simply use your login credentials for immediate access.

Table of Contents

Preface	**1**
Chapter 1: Time to Prototype	**5**
Rough wireframing and prototypying	**6**
Prototyping smaller projects	8
Prototyping wrap-up	8
Introducing the framework	**9**
Going over the base theme	**10**
Referring to the Foundation documentation	**13**
Migrating to a newer version of Foundation	**13**
Framework support	14
Browser support	14
Extending Foundation	15
Overview of our one-page demo website	15
Summary	**16**
Chapter 2: The Foundation Grid	**17**
The Foundation grid basics	**19**
Centering columns in the grid	**21**
Offsetting the grid	**22**
The block grid	**23**
Nesting the grid	**24**
Setting element position based on screen size	**25**
Modifying the base theme and building a demo site	**26**
Summary	**29**
Chapter 3: Navigation	**31**
The simple top navigation bar	**31**
Navigation tweaks	**36**
Side navigation	38

Subnavigation	38
Breadcrumbs	38
Pagination	**39**
Let's navigate together	**40**
Summary	**45**
Chapter 4: Elements	**47**
Typography	**48**
Subheadings	48
The small tag	49
Lists	**49**
Inline lists	50
Definition lists	51
Blockquote	**51**
V-cards	**52**
Buttons	**52**
Drop-down buttons	53
Drop-down buttons with images and text	54
Split drop-down buttons	55
Button groups	55
Panels	**57**
Pricing tables	**60**
Pricing tables in columns	61
Pricing tables in columns without a gutter	61
Fixing border issues	62
Tables	**63**
Video	**64**
Progress bars	**64**
Keystrokes	**65**
Label	**65**
Print styles	65
Sliders	65
Alerts	68
Tooltips	68
Utility	69
Visibility	70
Switches	72
The icon bar	72
Summary	**73**

Chapter 5: JavaScript   75

Magellan sticky navigation   77
    Magellan sticky navigation code explanation   80
Off-canvas navigation   80
Interchange responsive content   83
    Interchange responsive default content   86
    Interchange responsive images   86
    Interchange responsive images with media queries   87
    Interchange responsive background images   87
    Retina media queries   87
Orbit slider   88
Clearing   90
Forms   91
Form validation   94
Reveal   95
Joyride   96
Accordion   97
Tabs   99
Summary   100

Chapter 6: Testing   101

Testing IE 6-11   101
Supporting unsupported versions of IE   106
    Testing IE7 and IE6   107
Multiple device testing   107
    Remote debugging   108
    Chrome simulation   108
    Other tools you can try out for testing purposes   111
Summary   111

Chapter 7: Sass and Foundation   113

Introducing Sass   114
Installing Foundation with Sass   116
Going over the default settings file   121
Covering the variables   123
Going over the files   130
The index file   131
How do my files get converted?   132
What is Grunt?   132

Why is the setup so complicated?   133
Let's review the JS files   133
Summary   134

Chapter 8: Mixins   **135**
What are mixins?   135
Using a mixin within Sass and Foundation   139
Mixin libraries and other useful mixins   144
Summary   144

Chapter 9: Designing Responsive Ideas   **145**
Using Foundation for in-browser designs   145
Building a quick prototype   148
Reviewing the prototype   153
Customizing the prototype   155
Foundation theme   177
Creating Foundation grids in Photoshop   177
Summary   178

Chapter 10: Foundation with Other Tools   **179**
Finding a starter theme   179
Using Foundation with other frameworks   184
Ideas on how to play nice with developers   184
Summary   187
Where to go from here   187

Index   **189**

Preface

First off, thanks for purchasing this book. I am grateful that I have the opportunity to write a book on a framework that I have loved and used for the last four years! This book starts off with teaching you the basics of Zurb Foundation, and gradually moves on to cover the most advanced parts of this amazing framework. You will learn how to use Foundation to prototype, design, and theme a website using any programming language or content management system.

What this book covers

Chapter 1, Time to Prototype, covers how to wireframe and prototype with Foundation. Foundation is really fast and you can get a clickable prototype to show your clients on multiple devices and platforms.

Chapter 2, The Foundation Grid, gives an overview of the grid sizes and covers how to use them to lay out your projects.

Chapter 3, Navigation, covers how to use the different types of navigation.

Chapter 4, Elements, describes how to add and theme elements in our site; this is where you will learn a lot of things that can be reused in all your Foundation projects in the future. We will talk about how to override and add attributes to make our own customized responsive theme.

Chapter 5, JavaScript, covers how to use and theme the JavaScript libraries.

Chapter 6, Testing, explains how to perform cross-browser and device testing when doing responsive design and development.

Chapter 7, Sass and Foundation, gives a quick Sass overview on how to install the Foundation Sass version and use it in your projects.

Chapter 8, Mixins, covers what mixins are and how to use them with Foundation

Chapter 9, Designing Responsive Ideas, explains responsive design ideas and gives you some ideas of what to think about when you are designing.

Chapter 10, Foundation with Other Tools, covers how to use Foundation with content management systems and other custom programming languages.

What you need for this book

I am going to assume a few things about what you should know before starting this book:

- You should at least have basic knowledge of HTML, CSS, and should have used JavaScript. I do not expect you to know how to code JavaScript, just that you are comfortable implementing it in a project.
- You should use Chrome.
- You should be able to use a Mac, Windows, Linux, or Chrome OS for this book.
- You will need an editor; I like Sublime Text myself. You can download a free trial from `http://www.sublimetext.com/`. I am also a fan of PHPStorm; you can also get a free trial from `http://www.jetbrains.com`. If you have another editor you like, go ahead and use it. If you want to use a really good free online editor that will work in your browser including Chrome OS, you can use `https://codio.com/`.

Who this book is for

This book is for anyone who wants to learn responsive web design using the most advanced responsive framework, Zurb Foundation. You can be a designer, developer, or a combination of both.

Conventions

In this book, you will find a number of styles of text that distinguish between different kinds of information. Here are some examples of these styles and an explanation of their meaning.

Code words in text, database table names, folder names, filenames, file extensions, pathnames, dummy URLs, user input, and Twitter handles are shown as follows: "The foundation.min.js file is a minified version of all the files in the Foundation folder."

A block of code is set as follows:

```
<div class="row">
  <div class="small-12 medium-6 large-4 columns">Column One</div>
  <div class="small-12 medium-6 large-4 columns">Column Two</div>
  <div class="small-12 medium-6 large-4 columns">Column Three</div>
</div>
```

New terms and **important words** are shown in bold. Words that you see on the screen, in menus or dialog boxes for example, appear in the text like this: "Then, refresh your browser and you should see just the **Learning Zurb Foundation** title."

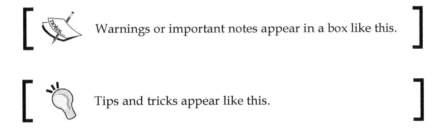

Warnings or important notes appear in a box like this.

Tips and tricks appear like this.

Reader feedback

Feedback from our readers is always welcome. Let us know what you think about this book—what you liked or may have disliked. Reader feedback is important for us to develop titles that you really get the most out of.

To send us general feedback, simply send an e-mail to feedback@packtpub.com, and mention the book title through the subject of your message.

If there is a topic that you have expertise in and you are interested in either writing or contributing to a book, see our author guide on www.packtpub.com/authors.

Customer support

Now that you are the proud owner of a Packt book, we have a number of things to help you to get the most from your purchase.

Downloading the example code

You can download the example code files for all Packt books you have purchased from your account at http://www.packtpub.com. If you purchased this book elsewhere, you can visit http://www.packtpub.com/support and register to have the files e-mailed directly to you.

Errata

Although we have taken every care to ensure the accuracy of our content, mistakes do happen. If you find a mistake in one of our books—maybe a mistake in the text or the code—we would be grateful if you would report this to us. By doing so, you can save other readers from frustration and help us improve subsequent versions of this book. If you find any errata, please report them by visiting http://www.packtpub.com/support, selecting your book, clicking on the **errata submission form** link, and entering the details of your errata. Once your errata are verified, your submission will be accepted and the errata will be uploaded to our website, or added to any list of existing errata, under the Errata section of that title.

Piracy

Piracy of copyright material on the Internet is an ongoing problem across all media. At Packt, we take the protection of our copyright and licenses very seriously. If you come across any illegal copies of our works, in any form, on the Internet, please provide us with the location address or website name immediately so that we can pursue a remedy.

Please contact us at copyright@packtpub.com with a link to the suspected pirated material.

We appreciate your help in protecting our authors, and our ability to bring you valuable content.

Questions

You can contact us at questions@packtpub.com if you are having a problem with any aspect of the book, and we will do our best to address it.

1
Time to Prototype

Over the last couple of years, showing wireframes to most clients has not really worked well for me. They never seem to quite get it, and if they do, they never seem to fully understand all the functionality through a wireframe. For some people, it is really hard to picture things in their head, they need to see exactly what it will look and function like to truly understand what they are looking at. You should still do a rough wireframe either on paper, on a whiteboard, or on the computer. Then once you and/or your team are happy with these rough wireframes, then jump right into the prototype.

We will be covering the following points in this chapter:

- How to move away from showing clients wireframes and how to create responsive prototypes
- Why these prototypes are better and quicker than doing traditional wireframes
- The different versions of Foundation
- What does Foundation include?
- How to use the documentation
- How to migrate from an older version
- Getting support when you can't figure something out
- What browsers does Foundation support?
- How to extend Foundation
- Our demo site

Rough wireframing and prototypping

You might think prototyping this early on when the client has only seen a sitemap is crazy, but the thing is, once you master Foundation, you can build prototypes in about the same time you would spend doing traditional high quality wireframes in Illustrator or whatever program you currently use. With these prototypes, you can make things clickable, interactive, and super fast to make edits to after you get feedback from the client. With the default Foundation components, you can work out how things will work on a phone, tablet, and desktop/laptop. This way you can work with your team to fully understand how things will function and start seeing where the project's potential issues will be. You can then assign people to start dealing with these potential problems early on in the process.

When you are ready to show the client, you can walk them through their project on multiple devices and platforms. You can easily show them what content they are going to need and how that content will flow and reflow based on the medium the user is viewing their project on. You should try to get content as early as possible; a lot of companies are hiring content strategists. These content strategists handle working with the client to get, write, and rework content to fit in the responsive web medium. This allows you to design around a client's content, or at least some of the content. We all know that what a client says they will get you for content is not always what you get, so you may need to tweak the design to fit the actual content you get. Making these theming changes to accommodate these content changes can be a pain, but with Foundation, you can just reflow part of the page and try some ideas out in the prototype before you put them back into the working development site. Once you have built up a bunch of prototypes, you can easily combine and use parts of them to create new designs really fast for current or new projects.

When prototyping, you should keep everything grayscale, without custom fonts, or a theme beyond the base Foundation one. These prototypes do not have to look pretty. The less it looks like a full design, the better off you will be. You will have to inform your client that an actual design for their project will be coming and that it will be done after they sign off this prototype.

When you show the client, you should bring a phone, a tablet, and a laptop to show them how the project will flow on each of these devices. This takes out all the confusion about what happens to the layouts on different screen sizes and on touch and non-touch devices. It also allows your client and your team to fully understand what they are building and how everything works and functions.

Trying to take a PDF of wireframes, a Photoshop file, and trying to piece them together to build a responsive web project can be really challenging. With this approach, so many details can get lost in translation, you have to keep going back to talk to the client or your team about how certain things should work or function. Even worse, you have to make huge changes to a section close to the end of the project because something was designed without being really thought through and now your developers have to scramble to make something work within the budget. Prototyping can sort out all the issues or at least the major issues that could arise in the project.

With these Foundation prototypes, you keep building on the code for each step of the web building process. Your designer can work with your frontend/backend team to come up with a prototype that everyone is happy with and commit to being able to build it before the client sees anything. If you are familiar with version control, you can use it to keep track of your prototypes and collaborate with another person or a team of people. The two most popular version control software applications are Git (http://git-scm.com/) and Subversion (http://subversion.apache.org/). Git is the more popular of the two right now; however, if you are working on a project that has been around for a number of years, chances are that it will be in Subversion. You can migrate from one to the other, but it might take a bit of work.

These prototypes keep your team on the same page right from the beginning of the project and allow the client to sign off on functionality and how the project will work on different mediums. Yes, you are spending more time at the beginning getting everyone on the same page and figuring out functionality early on, but this process should sort out all the confusion later in a project and save you time and money at the end of the project.

When the client has changes that are out of scope, it is easy to reference back to the prototype and show them how that change will impact what they signed off on. If the change is major enough then you will need to get them a cost on making that change happen.

You should test your prototypes on an iPhone, an Android phone, an iPad, and your desktop or laptop. I would also figure out what browser your client uses and make sure you test on that as well. If they are using an older version of IE, 8 or earlier, you will need to have the conversation with them about how Foundation 4+ does not support IE8. If that support is needed, you will have to come up with a solution to handle this outdated version of IE. We will talk about some ideas on how to do this in a later chapter. Looking at a client's analytics to see what versions of IE their clients are coming to the project with will help you decide how to handle older versions of IE. Analytics might tell you that you can drop the version all together.

Another great component that is included with Foundation is Modernizr (http://modernizr.com/); this allows you to write conditional JS and/or CSS for a specific situation or browser version. This really can be a lifesaver. Learning more about Modernizr is out of scope for this book, but you can use it with or without Foundation.

Prototyping smaller projects

While you are learning Foundation, you might think that using Foundation on a smaller project will eat up your entire budget. However, these are the best projects to learn Foundation. Basically, you take the prototype to a place where you can show a client the rough look and feel using Foundation. Then, you create a theme board in Photoshop with colors, fonts, photos and anything else to show the client. This first version will be a grayscale prototype that will function across multiple screen sizes. Then you can pull up your theme board to show the direction you are thinking of for the look and feel. If you still feel more comfortable doing your designs in Photoshop, there are some really good Photoshop grid templates at http://www.yeedeen.com/downloads/category/30-psd. If you want to create a custom grid that you can take a screenshot of, then paste into Photoshop, and then drag your guidelines over the grid to make your own template, you can refer to http://www.gridlover.net/foundation/.

Prototyping wrap-up

These methods are not perfect and may not always work for you, but you're going to see my workflow and how Foundation can be used on all of your web projects. You will figure out what will work with your clients, your projects, and your workflow. Also, you might have slightly different workflows based on the type of project, and/or project budget.

If the client does not see value in having a responsive site, you should choose if you want to work with these types of clients. The Web is not one standard resolution anymore and it never will be again, so if a client does not understand that, you might want to consider not working with them. These types of clients are usually super hard to work with and your time is better spent on clients that get or are willing to allow you to teach them and trust you that you are building their project for the modern Web. Personally, clients that have fought with me to not be responsive usually come back a few months later wondering why their site does not work great on their new smartphone or tablet and wanting you to fix it. So try and address this up front and it will save you grief later on and make your clients happier and their experience better.

Like anything, there are exceptions to this but just make sure you have a contract in place to outline that you are not building this as responsive, and that it could cause the client a lot of grief and costs later to go back and make it responsive. No matter what you do for a client, you should have a contract in place, this will just make sure you both understand what is each party responsible for. Personally, I like to use a modified version of, (https://gist.github.com/malarkey/4031110). This contract does not have any legal mumbo jumbo that people do not understand. It is written in plain English and has a little bit of a less serious tone.

Now that we have covered why prototyping with Foundation is faster than doing wireframes or prototypes in Photoshop, let's talk about what comes in the base Foundation framework. Then we will cover which version to install, and then go through each file and folder.

Introducing the framework

Before we get started, please refer to the http://foundation.zurb.com/develop/download.html webpage.

You will see that there are four versions of Foundation: complete, essentials, custom, and SCSS. We will be using the complete version for the first parts of this book. But let's talk about the other versions. The essentials is just a smaller version of Foundation that does not include all the components of the framework; this version is a barebones version. Once you are familiar with Foundation, you will likely only include the components that you need for a specific project. By only including the components you need, you can speed up the load time of your project and you do not make the user download files that are not being used by your project. The custom version allows you to pick the components and basic sizes, colors, radius, and text direction. You will likely use this or the SCSS version of Foundation once you are more comfortable with the framework.

The SCSS or Sass version of Foundation is the most powerful version. If you do not know what Sass is, it basically gives you additional features of CSS that can speed up how you theme your projects. We will be covering Sass later in this book. There is actually another version of Foundation that is not listed on this page, which can be found by hitting the blue **Getting Started** option in the top right-corner and then clicking on **App Guide** under **Building and App**. You can also visit this version at http://foundation.zurb.com/docs/applications.html. This version is the Ruby Gem version of Foundation, and unless you are building a Ruby on Rails project, you will never use this version of Foundation. Zurb keeps the gem pretty up to date, you will likely get the new version of the **gem** about a week or two after the other versions come out.

There are other versions of Foundation that people have ported to other languages, frameworks, and content management systems, and we will cover some of these at the end of this book.

Alright, let's get into Foundation. If you have not already, hit the blue **Download Everything** button below the complete heading on the webpage.

We will be building a one page demo site from the base Foundation theme that you just downloaded. This way, you can see how to take what you are given by default and customize this base theme to look anyway you want it to. We will give this base theme a custom look and feel, and make it look like you are not using a responsive framework at all. The only way to tell is if you view the source of the website. The Zurb components have very little theming applied to them. This allows you to not have to worry about really overriding the CSS code and you can just start adding additional CSS to customize these components.

We will cover how to use all the major components of the framework and by the end of the book, you will have an advanced understanding of the framework and how you can use it on all your projects going forward. The idea of this book is to give you a real-life example and show you how you can manipulate the framework to build any type of web project or app that you throw at it. Foundation has been used on small-to-large websites, web apps, at startups, with content management systems, and with enterprise-level applications.

Going over the base theme

The base theme that you download is made up of an HTML index file, a folder of CSS files, JavaScript files, and an empty img folder for images, which are explained in the following points:

- The index.html file has a few Foundation components to get you started. You have three, 12- column grids at three screen sizes; small, medium, and large. If this does not make sense right now, that is fine, when we start getting into the grid in the next chapter, it will make sense then. You can also control how many columns are in the grid, and the spacing (also called the gutter) between the columns, and how to use the other grid options. We will cover all of this in the next chapter. You will soon notice that you have full control over pretty much anything and you can control how things are rendered on any screen size or device, and whether that device is in portrait or landscape. You also have the ability to render different code on different devices and for different screen sizes.

- In the CSS folder, there is the un-minified version of Foundation with the filename `foundation.css`. There is also a minified version of Foundation with the filename `foundation.min.css`. If you are not familiar with minification, it has the same code as the `foundation.css` file, just all the spacing, comments, and code formatting have been taken out. This makes the file really hard to read and edit, but the file size is smaller and will speed up your project's load time. Most of the time, minified files have all the code on one really long line. You should use the `foundation.css` file as reference but actually include the minified one in your project. The minified version makes debugging and error fixing almost impossible, so we use the un-minified version for development and then the minified version for production.

- The last file in that folder is `normalize.css`; this file can be called a reset file, but it is more of an alternative to a reset file. This file is used to try to set defaults on a bunch of CSS elements and tries to get all the browsers to be set to the same defaults. The thinking behind this is that every browser will look and render things the same, and, therefore, there should not be a lot of specific theming fixes for different browsers. These types of files do a pretty good job but are not perfect and you will have to do little fixes for different browsers, even the modern ones. We will also cover how to use some extra CSS to take resetting certain elements a little further than the normalize file does for you. This will mainly include showing you how to render form elements and buttons to be the same across-browser and device. We will also talk about, browser version, platform, OS, and screen resolution detection when we talk about testing.

- We will also be adding our own CSS file that we will add our customizations to, so if you ever decide to update the framework as a new version comes out, you will not have to worry about overriding your changes. We will never add or modify the core files of the framework; I highly recommend you do not do this either. Once we get into Sass, we will cover how you can really start customizing the framework defaults using the custom variables that are built right into Foundation. These variables are one of the reasons that Foundation is the most advanced responsive framework out there. These variables are super powerful and one of my favorite things about Foundation. Once you understand how to use variables, you can write your own or you can extend your setup of Foundation as much as you like.

- In the JS folder, you will find a few files and some folders. In the Foundation folder, you will find each of the JavaScript components that you need to make Foundation work properly cross-device, browser, and responsive. These JavaScript components can also be use to extend Foundation's functionality even further. You can only include the components that you need in your project. This allows you to keep the framework lean and can help with load times; this is especially useful on mobile. You can also use CSS to theme each of these components to be rendered differently on each device or at different screen sizes.

- The `foundation.min.js` file is a minified version of all the files in the Foundation folder. You can decide based on your needs whether you want to include only the JavaScripts you are using on that project or whether you want to include them all. When you are learning, you should include them all. When you are comfortable with the framework and are ready to make your project live, you should only include the JavaScripts you are actually using. This helps with load times and can make troubleshooting easier. Many of the Foundation components will not work without including the JavaScript for that component.

- The next file you will notice is `jquery.js` it might be either in the root of this folder or in the vendor folder if you are using a newer version of Foundation 5. If you are not familiar with jQuery, it is a JavaScript library that makes DOM manipulation, event handling, animation, and Ajax a lot easier. It also makes all of this stuff work cross-browser and cross-device.

- The next file in the JS folder or in the `vendor` folder under JS is `modernizr.js`; this file helps you to write conditional JavaScript and/or CSS to make things work **cross-browser** and to make progressive enhancements. We will cover this more when we talk about testing in a later chapter.

- Also, you put third-party JavaScript libraries that you are using on your project in the vendor folder. These are libraries that you either wrote yourself or found online, are not part of Foundation, and are not required for Foundation to work properly. There are a few others in there currently; we will not be covering them in the book, but just know that they are needed by the framework and you will not really need to ever touch them.

Referring to the Foundation documentation

The Foundation documentation is located at `http://foundation.zurb.com/docs/`.

Foundation is really well documented and provides a lot of code samples and examples to use in your own projects. All the components also contain Sass variables that you can use to customize some of the defaults and even build your own. This saves you writing a bunch of override CSS classes.

Each part of the framework is listed on the left-hand side and you can click on what you are looking for. You are taken to a page about that specific part and can read the section's overview, view code samples, working examples, and how to customize that part of the framework. Each section has a pretty good walk through about how to use each piece.

Zurb is constantly updating Foundation, so you should check the change log every once in a while at `http://foundation.zurb.com/docs/changelog.html`.

If you need documentation on an older version of Foundation, it is at the bottom of the documentation site in the left-hand column. Zurb keeps all the documentation back to Foundation 2. The only reason you will ever need to use Foundation 2 is if you need to support a really, really old version of IE, such as version 7. Foundation never supported IE6, but you will likely never have to worry about that version of IE.

Migrating to a newer version of Foundation

If you have an older version of Foundation, each version has a migration guide. The migration guide from Foundation 4 to 5 can be found at `http://foundation.zurb.com/docs/upgrading.html`.

Personally, I have migrated websites and web apps in multiple languages and as long as Zurb does not change the grid, like they did from Foundation 3 to 4, then usually we copy-and-paste over the old version of the Foundation CSS, JavaScript, and images. You will likely have to change some JavaScript calls, do some testing, and do some minor fixes here and there, but it is usually a pretty smooth process as long as you did not modify the core framework or write a bunch of custom overrides. If you did either of these things, you will be in for a lot of work or a full rebuild of your project, so you should never modify the core.

For old versions of Foundation, or if your version has been heavily modified, it might be easier to start with a fresh version of Foundation and copy-and-paste in the parts that you want to still use. Personally, I have done both and it really depends on the project.

Before you do any migration, make sure you are using some sort of version control, such as GIT. If you do not know what GIT is, you should look into it. Here is a good place to start: (http://git-scm.com/book/en/Getting-Started) GIT has saved me from losing code so many times. If GIT is a little overwhelming right now, at the very least, duplicate your project folder as a backup and then copy in the new version of the framework over your files. If things are really broken, you can at least still use your old version while you work out the kinks in the new version.

Framework support

At some point, you will likely have questions about something in the framework, or will be trying to get something to work and for some reason, you can't figure it out. Foundation has multiple ways to get support, some of which are listed as follows:

- E-mail
- Twitter
- GitHub
- StackOverflow
- Forums

To visit or get in-touch with support go to http://foundation.zurb.com/support/support.html.

Browser support

Foundation 5 supports the majority of browsers and devices, but like anything modern, it drops support for older browser versions. If you need IE8 or cringe, or IE7 support, you will need to use an older version of Foundation. You can see a full browser and device compatibility list at http://foundation.zurb.com/docs/compatibility.html.

Extending Foundation

Zurb also builds a bunch of other components that usually make their way into Foundation at some point, and work well with Foundation even though they are not officially part of it. These components range from new JavaScript libraries, fonts, icons, templates, and so on. You can visit their playground at `http://zurb.com/playground`. This playground also has other great resources and tools that you can use on other projects and other mediums. The things at Zurb's playground can make designing with Foundation a lot easier, even if you are not a designer. It can take quite a while to find icons or make them into SVGs or fonts for use in your projects, but Zurb has provided these in their playground.

Overview of our one-page demo website

The best way to show you how to learn the Zurb Foundation Responsive Framework is to actually get you building a demo site along with me. You can visit the final demo site we will be building at `http://www.learningzurbfoundation.com/demo`. You can also view each chapter on GitHub at `https://github.com/kevinhorek/Learning-Zurb-Foundation`. Also, I will keep posting each chapter's code in a folder at `https://codio.com/kevinhorek/Learning-Zurb-Foundation`; this is a free online IDE, so you can play with the actual code in the browser, clone it, and even preview the site in your own browser.

We will be taking the base starter theme that we downloaded and making a one-page demo site. The demo site is built to teach you how to use the components and how they work together. You can also add outside components, but you can try those on your own. The demo site will show you how to build a responsive website, and it might not look like an ideal site, but I am trying to use as many components as possible to show you how to use the framework. Once you complete this site, you will have a deep understanding of the framework. You can then use this site as a starter theme or at the very least, as a reference for all your Foundation projects going forward.

Summary

In this chapter, we covered how to rough wireframe and quickly moved into prototyping. We also covered the following points:

- We went over what is included in the base Foundation theme
- Explored the documentation and how to migrate Foundation versions
- How to get framework support
- Started to get you thinking about browser support
- Letting you know that you can extend Foundation beyond its defaults
- We quickly covered our one-page demo site

In the next chapter, we will drive into the grid!

2
The Foundation Grid

By default, HTML and CSS do not have a grid or a really good cross-browser way to lay web projects out. This is why responsive grid frameworks, such as Foundation, have been created. They allow you to extend the core of these languages and really speed up your development time.

We will cover the following topics in this chapter:

- The Foundation grid basics
- Centering in the grid
- Offsetting the grid
- The block grid
- Nesting the grid
- Setting element position based on screen size
- Modifying the base theme and building a demo site

At a high level, the main purpose of Foundation is to start you off with a responsive grid that will allow you to layout simple to the most complex web layouts that work on any screen size. Foundation allows you to have full control over each column and row on small, medium, and large screen sizes. If you want to tweak any element, column, or row on a screen of any size, you can add custom media queries to pretty much anything. For those of you who do not know what media queries are, they are CSS tags that allow you to set screen sizes' ranges for certain CSS attributes to be applied at those ranges. These ranges are usually phone, table, and desktop/laptop screen sizes. This way, you can have control over how your project looks at these screen sizes. We will be covering media queries a few times throughout this book.

You should never edit the base grid files as this can cause you grave issues while updating the layouts. Instead, you should override or change the grid in your own CSS file, so as Zurb updates Foundation, you do not have to worry about overriding your changes.

Foundation has three 12-column grids that are targeted at three types of screen sizes: small, medium, and large. Each of these grid sizes have default ranges; these can be changed or you can even add more or less columns, but for our purposes right now, we will use the default sizes. You are likely to use all three of the grid sizes on any project you want to be responsive. The idea is that you code for small screens first and as the screen size gets bigger, the project inherits the small screen styles and you can add more customizations for larger screens. For example, on small screens, you let your buttons just have a solid color, but on medium and large screens, you add in CSS gradients and some text shadow. Not having these CSS effects rendered on a mobile can speed up the time taken to load a page. You need to balance design with the time taken to load pages and brand for the three main screen sizes. Also, you need to consider that if you do not need your project to be responsive and do not test your project for the other screen sizes, your site will look broken at certain resolutions.

Thinking about making the mobile design of a site first is a really new concept and can be really hard to wrap your head around, especially while trying to show a client the mobile version before the desktop version. So, we will take a slightly different approach. A small grid works better on larger screens than a large grid does on a small screen. So, what we will do is get all the basic elements, content, text, and images into the small and large grids and lay out how we want it to look like at these two screen sizes. All the formatting, colors, text, and CSS do not need to be in yet, just the general layout. You should also perform some quick testing on devices at this point as well. You should also be testing the two grid sizes, by just resizing your browser window from large to small and back to large.

You will see the different grid sizes kick in. The different grid sizes are basically just media query ranges. Most of the people who visit your web projects do not resize their browser window when surfing the Web, but this is a quick way to see how things are coming together at different screen sizes and while triggering different grids. We not only need to think of this approach as mobile first, but also need to think about how things will look on a larger screen at the same time and then sort out what happens in between these two screen size ranges with the medium grid. Your elements will likely start stacking on top of each other as you get down to the smaller screen sizes. These same elements can also and will change positions at different grid sizes.

We will cover how to control this and even how to show something at one spot on a desktop but at a different spot on a tablet. This approach is easier for your team and the client to understand when presenting your prototypes; you can show them how their project will work and flow on large and small screens. You just need to make it clear that the medium or in-between state will be sorted out later in the project once they have signed off on the prototype.

The Foundation grid basics

The Foundation grid is made up of 12 columns at a maximum width of 62.5 rems and a gutter of 1.875 ems. If you are not familiar with ems, their explanation right from W3C (`http://dev.w3.org/csswg/css-values/#em-unit`) is:

> *"Equal to the computed value of the 'font-size' property of the element on which it is used."*

This way, everything scales with the font size. The gutter is the space between each column of the grid. You can set this to 0 or any value that you want. However, for this example, we will retain the default settings, and I will show you how to change all of these when we get into Sass later in this book. You can also change the maximum width of the grid. For most of my projects, I set it to 90 ems, but you can change it to whatever you like to suit your needs and we will cover how to do this later on.

Before the end of the chapter, let's get into the grid and talk about all the parts of the grid by starting on our one-page demo site. This demo site will cover everything that we will discuss in this book, and you can use it as a code reference in your future projects. We will be building a one-page prototype using as many of the Foundation components, so you get a really good hang of the framework.

The following is what one row looks like with three columns side by side on a large screen, two columns side by side on a medium screen, and three columns stacked on top of each other on a small screen:

```
<div class="row">
  <div class="small-12 medium-6 large-4 columns">Column One</div>
  <div class="small-12 medium-6 large-4 columns">Column Two</div>
  <div class="small-12 medium-6 large-4 columns">Column Three</div>
</div>
```

This might sound confusing at first, but let's break it apart and start with small-12. Each row you set on a div can contain up to 12 columns in that row for that screen size. So, for small screens, we are taking up all 12 columns with the 3 divs that have the copy of Column One. So, on a small screen, the div takes up the 12 columns, and the next column with the content Two Columns gets dropped down below Column One. The same thing happens with the third div with the content Column Three. Here is a diagram of how it renders on a small screen:

Column One
Column Two
Column Three

On a medium screen, this same code is rendered as follows:

Column One	Column Two
Column Three	

On a large screen, the same code would render like the following:

Column One	Column Two	Column Three

What you are looking to do is make each row have divs with grid sizes that add up to 12. There are ways to handle centering and not have a grid size add up to 12, but we will cover this shortly. Just for now, understand that for each size, you want the grid size to add up to 12. You also need to add the class columns after every column declaration, as shown in the previous code. This allows Foundation to handle a lot of the element reflow on different screen sizes. You also need to wrap these column divs in a div with a row class. This row class clears everything above and starts a new row on a new line; it also puts these 12 columns in a maximum width of 62.5 rems. Breaking things up into rows and columns is something that you need to think about throughout the design process.

The row class acts somewhat like a line break or clear:both in CSS; it moves everything to the next line and allows you to keep that content or columns contained inside that row and avoids overlapping any other rows or columns. If you add more than 12 columns to your row, you will get some stacking and/or unexpected results. We are building a prototype with both the small and large grid sizes so that you can see what your project will do and how it will flow on different screen sizes. This way, you can figure out design and development issues during the prototype phase, before the client has seen anything. This allows you to make big changes as early as possible in a project without really affecting anyone else involved in the project.

Grid templating tool

For a great tool to generate Foundation grids, you can try http://www.gridlover.net/foundation/. You can set up a custom grid in this tool, take a screenshot, and then change the grid numbers in your CSS or paste it in Photoshop and drag guides to accommodate this custom grid, and then start designing.

Centering columns in the grid

One of the most common things you would want to do is center a number of columns, and Foundation makes this really easy. You do this by adding the grid size and then -centered. So, to center your columns on a small screen, you will add the small-centered class. The following example shows you how to center eight columns on a small screen:

```
<div class="row">
  <div class="small-8 small-centered columns">3 centered</div>
</div>
```

Basically, it looks the same as how you would declare the small columns, but you just add the extra CSS class small-centered. If you do not want these columns centered on a large screen, add the large-uncentered class, as shown in the following code:

```
<div class="row">
  <div class="small-6 small-centered large-uncentered columns">6
centered on small but not on large</div>
</div>
```

As you can start to see, Foundation gives you a lot of control over the grid; let's cover some other grid features.

Offsetting the grid

Another thing you will likely need to do at some point is offset your columns. This is also really easy to do in Foundation. By making sure that your columns add up to 12 for a certain screen size, you can still add offsets to that screen size. So, let's try it out in the large grid:

```
<div class="row">
  <div class="large-2 columns">2 Columns</div>
  <div class="large-8 large-offset-2 columns">8 Columns, Offset by 2
Columns</div>
</div>
```

Here is what the rendered code will look like on the screen:

Two Columns	Column Two Offset	Eight Columns

As you can see, you have two columns, then you have a gap, an offset of two columns, and then you have another eight columns. Offsets are useful if you want to indent a section or put a space between sections, and they are a great way to start getting creative with the grid.

The block grid

Another great grid feature is the block grid; the block grid basically takes the elements and sets them to take up an equal amount of space across the row. You can specify how many columns will be at each grid size, as shown in the following code; this is really useful for the thumbnails under a gallery of images:

```
<ul class="small-block-grid-2 medium-block-grid-4 large-block-grid-6">
  <li><img src="image.jpg"></li>
  <li><img src="image.jpg"></li>
  <li><img src="image.jpg"></li>
  <li><img src="image.jpg"></li>
  <li><img src="image.jpg"></li>
  <li><img src="image.jpg"></li>
  <li><img src="image.jpg"></li>
  <li><img src="image.jpg"></li>
</ul>
```

Here is a diagram of how this will look on a medium screen:

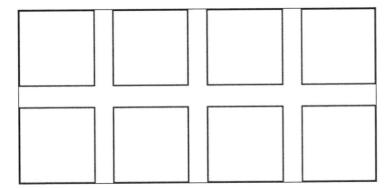

You can wrap this `ul` block grid in a `div` tag with a row class and create some very complex layouts.

Nesting the grid

One of the other powerful things you can do with the grid is nest the grid inside itself as many times as you like. For example, if you want to use all the 12 columns for the header and footer of your project, but you also want the middle content area to have a sidebar and a content area, you set the middle row to have 4 columns and 8 columns. This is fine because they add up to 12, but inside the 8 columns, you want to have an introductory paragraph that takes up the entire width. Under this paragraph, you want to have two columns of content. You would create another row with another with two columns of 6 divs. Here is how the code will look for the middle content area:

```
<div class="row">
  <div class="large-4 columns">Sidebar</div>
    <div class="large-8 columns">
    <p>Paragraph of content</p>
    <div class="row">
    <div class="large-6 columns">6 Columns</div>
    <div class="large-6 columns">6 Columns</div>
    </div>
  </div>
</div>
```

Here is a diagram of how this would look:

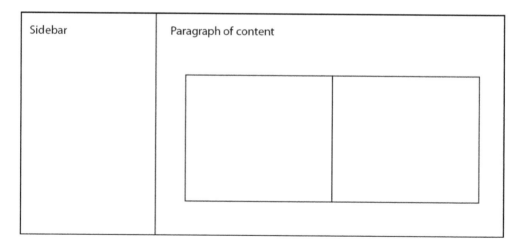

You can see that we are only setting how nesting will work on a large screen, but you can set how these columns will look on medium and small screens as well. Inside every two columns or more, you can nest another 12 columns. We will be nesting the grid throughout our one-page demo site, so we will cover nesting throughout this book.

Setting element position based on screen size

You might rarely need to use source ordering, but when you do, it is super handy, especially for SEO or other optimizations you want to perform for a certain screen size. Another example is when you want to show a sidebar on the left of the screen for medium and large screens, but on a small screen, you want that same navigation bar to be under your main content area. So, you will use source ordering to render the same code but display it differently on different screen sizes. This might not be the best design choice; you are likely to put your side menu on a small screen, in a drop-down menu, or a slide out menu, which appears at the left or the right of the screen. However, this is a simple example.

Source ordering can be really useful if you have a side navigation bar and some calls to actions in your sidebar. This is fine on large and medium screens, but what if you want to move the navigation elements into a drop-down or slide-out menu on a small screen and you want the calls to action below the content, as shown in the following diagrams. On a large screen, the diagram looks as follows:

Sidebar	Main Content

On a small screen, the diagram looks as follows:

Now that we have covered the grid, let's try what we just learned about the base Foundation theme. So, open your code editor and the Foundation files and let's get started.

Modifying the base theme and building a demo site

If you want to run the code along with me, you can see my code for each chapter on Codio at `https://codio.com/kevinhorek/Learning-Zurb-Foundation` or on Github at `https://github.com/kevinhorek/Learning-Zurb-Foundation`. First off, let's change the page titles in the `index.html` file on or around lines 7 and 16 to `Learning Zurb Foundation`. Next, let's delete lines 22 to 40, 46 to 150, and then delete lines 50 to 67. Then, refresh your browser and you should see just the **Learning Zurb Foundation** title.

So, we can see the grid at work. Let's add a border around our columns; we will remove this later. On line 9, let's add `<link rel="stylesheet" href="css/ foundation-book.css" />`, and then in our CSS folder, let's add a `foundation- book.css` file. In this CSS file, let's add the following code:

```
.columns {
    border: 1px solid black;
}
```

Next, perform the following:

1. On line 28, let's change `<div class="large-8 medium-8 columns">` to `<div class="small-12 medium-8 medium-push-4 large-8 large- push-4 columns">`.

2. On line 32, let's change `<div class="large-4 medium-4 columns">` to `<div class="small-12 medium-4 medium-pull-8 large-4 large-pull-8 columns">`.

3. On line 29, let's add `<p>Sidebar</p>`.

4. On line 33, let's add `<p>Content</p>`.

At this point, your code should look like this:

```
<!doctype html>
<html class="no-js" lang="en">

<head>
    <meta charset="utf-8" />
    <meta name="viewport" content="width=device-width, initial-
scale=1.0" />
    <title>Learning Zurb Foundation</title>
    <link rel="stylesheet" href="css/foundation.css" />
    <link rel="stylesheet" href="css/foundation-book.css" />
    <script src="js/modernizr.js"></script>
</head>

<body>

    <div class="row">
        <div class="large-12 columns">
            <h1>Learning Zurb Foundation</h1>
        </div>
    </div>

    <div class="row">
        <div class="large-12 columns">
```

```
        </div>
    </div>
    <div class="row">
        <div class="small-12 medium-8 medium-push-4 large-8 large-
push-4 columns">
            <p>Content</p>
        </div>

        <div class="small-12 medium-4 medium-pull-8 large-4 large-
pull-8 columns">
            <p>Sidebar</p>
        </div>
    </div>

    <script src="js/jquery.js"></script>
    <script src="js/foundation.min.js"></script>
    <script>
        $(document).foundation();
    </script>
</body>

</html>
```

So, now try resizing your browser. You will see that you have the sidebar on the left-hand side and content on the right, but when your window gets small, the content renders first and your sidebar is below the content. Pretty cool!

Now, let's change line 29 to the following:

```
<p>Paragraph of content</p>
<div class="row">
  <div class="small-8 small-centered medium-6 medium-uncentered
  large-6 columns">6 Columns or 8 small centered</div>
<div class="small-12 medium-6 large-6 columns">6 Columns or 12 small</
div>
</div>
```

Once you save and refresh your browser, resize it. You will see that you have nested columns and that on a large screen, you have a paragraph of content and 2 columns below this. When you resize your browser to a size that is small enough, you will see that your first 6 columns with the **6 Columns or 8 small centered** content is now taking up 8 of the 12 columns and is positioned at the center of your browser window. You will also notice that the second 6 columns with the **6 Columns or 12 small** content is taking up 12 columns on your screen. Also, you should see that your sidebar is still below all of this content.

Next, after line 39, hit the *Enter* key twice and type the following code:

```
<div class="row">
  <div class="large-2 columns">2 Columns</div>
  <div class="large-8 large-offset-2 columns">8 Columns, Offset by 2
Columns</div>
</div>
```

Now, go to your browser, refresh the page, and you will see 2 columns, then an offset of 2 columns, and then another 8 columns. If you resize your window to a medium or small size, you will see that that each of the columns just takes up all the 12 columns. You might wonder why this is so; this is because, if this is not set by default, your columns will just take up the full width of the screen. Go ahead and add small and medium grid sizes to your project.

Summary

In this chapter, we learned how to use the Foundation grid for multiple screen sizes, nesting the grid inside itself, using offsets and source ordering to help change how things look at different sizes, and how you can center the grid. In the next chapter, we will talk about the different navigation components that come with Foundation.

3
Navigation

Foundation has many navigation options that you can pick from to use in your web projects, so let's get into the basic elements and then we can build on those to create a truly dynamic navigation system. We will cover Foundation's navigation options and then we will put all the navigation types into our one-page demo site. Before that though, let's cover some of the elements first.

We will be covering the following points in this chapter:

- The simple top navigation bar
- Navigation tweaks
- Side navigation
- Subnavigation
- Breadcrumbs
- Pagination

We will try these elements together

The simple top navigation bar

The navigation bar consists of a `<nav>` element with a `"top-bar"` class applied to it. Nested within the `<nav>` element is a `<section>` element with a `"top-bar-section"` class applied. Finally, within the `<section>` element is an unordered list with a list of links.

Adding `"data-topbar"` to the `"nav"` element ensures that the top-bar functions correctly via JavaScript, as shown in the following code:

```
<nav class="top-bar" data-topbar>
    <section class="top-bar-section">
        <ul>
            <li><a href="#">Nav 1</a></li>
            <li><a href="#">Nav 2</a></li>
            <li><a href="#">Nav 3</a></li>
            <li><a href="#">Nav 4</a></li>
            <li><a href="#">Nav 5</a></li>
        </ul>
    </section>
</nav>
```

Next, we will give the first list item an active class; we do this by adding a `class="active"` class to our first `li` tag. You can see this in the following code:

```
<nav class="top-bar" data-topbar>
    <section class="top-bar-section">
        <ul>
            <li class="active"><a href="#">Nav 1</a></li>
            <li><a href="#">Nav 2</a></li>
            <li><a href="#">Nav 3</a></li>
            <li><a href="#">Nav 4</a></li>
            <li><a href="#">Nav 5</a></li>
        </ul>
    </section>
</nav>
```

Great! We have a working left-aligned menu, but what if we want to center this menu? We change a couple CSS attributes and the menu will be centered. We add a `"text-align: center"` attribute to our `"top-bar-section"` declaration and modify `ul` inside this class to be `"display: inline-block"` instead of just `"inline"`. The following are the CSS changes:

```
.top-bar-section {
    text-align: center;
}

.top-bar-section ul {
    display: inline-block;
}
```

This is a great start to a simple menu, but what if we want the first five navigational elements left aligned and we want to add a couple of elements on the right-hand side of this menu? First, we would remove the `text-align:center` declaration from our top-bar-section and create an additional unordered list after our first one and give that unordered list a class of right, as shown in the following code:

```
<nav class="top-bar" data-topbar>
  <section class="top-bar-section">
    <ul class="left">
      <li class="active"><a href="#">Nav 1</a></li>
      <li><a href="#">Nav 2</a></li>
      <li><a href="#">Nav 3</a></li>
      <li><a href="#">Nav 4</a></li>
      <li><a href="#">Nav 5</a></li>
    </ul>
    <ul class="right">
        <li><a href="#">Nav 6</a></li>
        <li><a href="#">Nav 7</a></li>
    </ul>
  </section>
</nav>
```

You will see that nav elements 6 and 7 will be right aligned, while nav elements 1 to 5 are still left aligned. The default alignment in Foundation is left, but you can customize Foundation to right align everything by default. We will cover this later on in the book.

Next we will give our navigation a title. Sometimes this is where you would swap out the tile for an image of a logo, but to keep it simple for now, let's just add a text title to our navigation. To do this, we add another unordered list, but this time we add it above the section tag. In the following code you will see that we give the ul a class of "`title-area`". Then you give the first li or the list item a class of "`name`". Then we have h1 with a link and inside that link you have the text for the logo, as shown in the following code:

```
<nav class="top-bar" data-topbar>
  <ul class="title-area">
    <li class="name">
      <h1><a href="#">Logo</a></h1>
    </li>
  </ul>
<section class="top-bar-section">
  <ul class="left">
    <li class="active"><a href="#">Nav 1</a></li>
```

```
        <li><a href="#">Nav 2</a></li>
        <li><a href="#">Nav 3</a></li>
        <li><a href="#">Nav 4</a></li>
        <li><a href="#">Nav 5</a></li>
    </ul>
    <ul class="right">
        <li><a href="#">Nav 6</a></li>
        <li><a href="#">Nav 7</a></li>
    </ul>
    </section>
</nav>
```

Great! We have a navigation bar with a logo and some left- and right-aligned elements, but what if we want to have a dropdown on one or all of the elements? This is pretty easy to achieve; we just add a class of `"has-dropdown"` to any of the list items. Let's try it on the `Nav 2 li` or the `list` element. Then after the Nav 2 link we add another unordered list with a class of `"dropdown"` and then we add the list and links and text links inside. Have a look at the following code:

```
<nav class="top-bar" data-topbar>
    <ul class="title-area">
        <li class="name">
            <h1><a href="#">Logo</a></h1>
        </li>
            </ul>
    <section class="top-bar-section">
        <ul class="left">
            <li class="active"><a href="#">Nav 1</a></li>
            <li class="has-dropdown">
                <a href="#">Nav 2</a>
            <ul class="dropdown">
                <li><a href="#">Nav 2.1</a></li>
                <li><a href="#">Nav 2.2</a></li>
                <li><a href="#">Nav 2.3</a></li>
                <li><a href="#">Nav 2.4</a></li>
            </ul>
            </li>
            <li><a href="#">Nav 3</a></li>
            <li><a href="#">Nav 4</a></li>
            <li><a href="#">Nav 5</a></li>
        </ul>
        <ul class="right">
            <li><a href="#">Nav 6</a></li>
            <li><a href="#">Nav 7</a></li>
```

```
    </ul>
  </section>
</nav>
```

If you want to add a dropdown inside of a dropdown, you just add it inside of the li you want to have the third level, just like we did in the li `Nav 2` list element.

Right now, the dropdowns are working on hover; hover does not work on a touch device, and Foundation will automatically make any of your hover states into clickable ones on a touch device. Let's say you want to remove the hover state and make these dropdowns be on click instead on a large screen. You can do this by adding a data option attribute to your `nav` tag right after `"data-topbar"`. You also need to add the data option; you can do this by adding `"data-options=is_ hover:false"`:

```
<nav class="top-bar" data-topbar data-options="is_hover: false">
```

Prefect! We have a working menu but what about a mobile version of this same menu? We can't have seven navigation elements span across a phone screen in one line, so we need to add one last thing to the menu to get it working on a small screen. Right after the h1 logo li, we need to add another li with a class of `"toggle-topbar menu icon"` and a couple other small things, as shown in the following code:

```
<ul class="title-area">
    <li class="name">
        <h1><a href="#">Logo</a></h1>
    </li>
    <li class="toggle-topbar menu-icon"><a href="#"><span>Nav</span></a></li>
</ul>
```

This will hide all seven menu items and turn them into a dropdown under the **Nav** text, as shown in the following diagram:

Logo		Nav
Logo		Nav
		Nav 1
		Nav 2

Now, we will have a menu that works on all screen sizes and when the menu is too long for the screen size, it will automatically be converted to a dropdown menu and the Nav 1-7 will be stacked on top of each other. If there is a third level like we added on the **Nav 2** element, it will be clickable. When you click on this **Nav 2** element, it will slide to the next level of navigation and the first element in this level will be a back button. The following is what your navigation will look like:

```
Back
Nav 2.1
Nav 2.2
Nav 2.3
Nav 2.4
```

There you have it; we just covered how to set up a basic navigation bar and then add it to transform it into a responsive menu with dropdowns that works on any screen size! This is a great starting point, and we will include this in our one-page site, so if this does not make complete sense right now, do not worry. If you want to refer to the sample, you can visit `https://codio.com/kevinhorek/Learning-Zurb-Foundation/tree/Chapter-3/index.html` and the navigation starts on line 15.

Navigation tweaks

Now, let's say we just put the navigation bar at the very top of our page and outside of the Foundation framework. This will cause the navigation bar to take 100 percent width of the browser window and it is the first element on the page, as shown in the following diagram:

If you want to make the navbar stay at the top of the user's screen while scrolling, you can create a "sticky" navigation bar (or any other element you want) by simply wrapping the desired element in a `<div>` tag with a class of "fixed" applied. Have a look at the following code example:

```
<div class="fixed">
  <nav class="top-bar" data-topbar>
    *** Menu ul's would be here ***
  </nav>
</div>
```

We can also set the navbar to not be 100 percent of the window, as shown in the following figure:

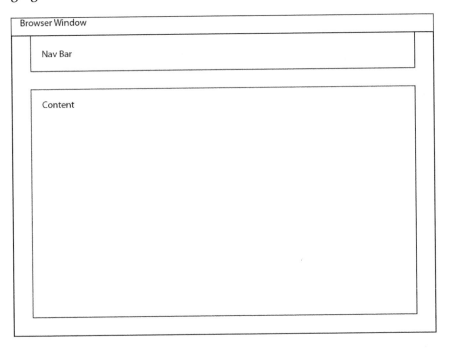

We do this by adding a "contain-to-grid" class to the div that already has the "fixed" class on it, as shown in the following code:

```
<div class="fixed contain-to-grid">
  <nav class="top-bar" data-topbar >
    ***  Menu ul's would be here ***
  </nav>
</div>
```

Side navigation

If you are building a site that uses side navigation, then Foundation has you covered. It is really simple to use: you just create a `<ul>` element, and give it a class of `"side-nav"` and add some list items with links and you will have a basic side menu that will stack each item on top of each other. If you want a horizontal divider between each menu item, you just add another li with the class of `"divider"` between the elements. Refer to the following code:

```
<ul class="side-nav">
  <li class="active"><a href="#">Side Nav 1</a></li>
  <li class="divider"></li>
  <li><a href="#">Side Nav 2</a></li>
</ul>
```

Subnavigation

When you are looking for an easy way to layout a filter or sort by an element, you can use a definition list with the `"sub-nav"` class. If you want a title for this subnavigation add a dt option, which is a definition title element with title text. In the following code, you will see that we are using Sort by: as the title of the definition list. You can also add an active class; this will show the user that they are sorting by that attribute. In the following code, you will see that Oldest is currently active and this shows the user that they are sorting by the oldest:

```
<dl class="sub-nav">
  <dt>Sort By:</dt>
  <dd><a href="#">Newest</a></dd>
  <dd><a href="#">Unread</a></dd>
  <dd class="active"><a href="#">Oldest</a></dd>
  <dd><a href="#">Last</a></dd>
</dl>
```

Breadcrumbs

Breadcrumbs are pretty easy to use and the following code is basically just a `<nav>` tag with the class of `"breadcrumbs"` and then the links that will appear in the breadcrumb trail. If you don't want one of the breadcrumbs to be clickable, you add the class of `"unavailable"` to the `<a>` tag that don't want to be clickable. It will look like this: `<a href="#" class="unavailable">`. The `"unavailable"` class is generally used in tandem with `"current class"`. You will see we applied this class to the Nav 1 link.

If you want to show the current page that you are on, you add the "current" class, as shown in the following code. You can theme any of these classes how you like in your CSS. We will cover how to theme elements later on in this book, so do not worry about theming right now:

```
<nav class="breadcrumbs">
  <a href="#">Home</a>
  <a href="#" class="unavailable">Nav 1</a>
  <a href="#">Nav 1.2</a>
  <a href="#" class="current">Nav 1.2.1</a>
</nav>
```

When building a breadcrumb menu, you are not limited to using a `<nav>` element; you can replace the `<nav>` tag pair with a `<ul>` tag pair to achieve the same effect. However, the nav tag is more semantically correct, because you are creating a navigation element, so using the `<nav>` tag makes more sense.

Pagination

Another super useful component that Foundation provides is pagination. If you want your pagination to be "left align", just remove the "-centered" segment from the first div in the following code. But for most of your projects, you will want to "center" your pagination bar so you will likely use the following code. After you open div, use `<ul>` with the class of "pagination" and the first `<li>` has a class of "arrow", which renders "«", the double arrow pointing to the left. Keep in mind that classes are reusable. You can apply the "unavailable" class to your pagination bar's elements just like we did previously with our breadcrumb menu. You will see that the "unavailable" `<li>` item has the character code of "…"; this renders as three dots "...". These dots show that there are pages between 2 and 9. You will also notice a "current" class on the first li; this shows the current page you are on. At some point, the pagination bar will likely be generated dynamically using server-side script, but this is a great starting point for your pagination needs:

```
<div class="pagination-centered">
  <ul class="pagination">
    <li class="arrow unavailable"><a href="#">&laquo;</a></li>
    <li class="current"><a href="#">1</a></li> "
    <li><a href="#">2</a></li>
    <li class="unavailable"><a href="#">&hellip;</a></li>
    <li><a href="#">9</a></li>
    <li><a href="#">10</a></li>
    <li class="arrow"><a href="#">&raquo;</a></li>
  </ul>
</div>
```

Let's navigate together

Now that we have covered the basics of navigation, let's take it to the next level. We will try out the elements we just talked about, but also take things to the next level and add some advanced navigation to our one-page demo site. We'll start by adding a top navigation bar to our one pager. So let's delete lines 15-19 from chapter 2 and add the following code:

```
<nav class="top-bar" data-topbar data-options="is_hover: false">
    <ul class="title-area">
        <li class="name">
        <h1><a href="#">Logo</a></h1>
        </li>
        <li class="toggle-topbar menu-icon"><a href="#"><span>Nav</
span></a></li>
        </ul>
    <section class="top-bar-section">
      <ul class="left">
        <li class="active"><a href="#">Nav 1</a></li>
        <li class="has-dropdown">
          <a href="#">Nav 2</a>
          <ul class="dropdown">
            <li><a href="#">Nav 2.1</a></li>
            <li><a href="#">Nav 2.2</a></li>
            <li><a href="#">Nav 2.3</a></li>
            <li><a href="#">Nav 2.4</a></li>
          </ul>
          </li>
        <li><a href="#">Nav 3</a></li>
        <li><a href="#">Nav 4</a></li>
        <li><a href="#">Nav 5</a></li>
      </ul>
      <ul class="right">
        <li><a href="#">Nav 6</a></li>
        <li><a href="#">Nav 7</a></li>
      </ul>
    </section>
  </nav>
```

This is a combination of what we covered previously, but we can now see it actually working. Try the dropdown and resize your window to see the word "Nav" appear on the right. Try this dropdown, and you will see all your navigation in one clean dropdown.

Next, let's add a placeholder image that will represent a header. Add `<img src="http://placehold.it/1000x250">`, to line 45. So after your `nav` tag that we just added, you should have the following lines of code:

```
<div class="row">
    <div class="large-12 columns">
        <img src="http://placehold.it/1000x250">
    </div>
</div>
```

You will notice that you have a gray header image that says 1000 x 250, so try resizing your window to be a smaller size and watch how Foundation handles the image resizing for you, while still keeping the images aspect ratio. Pretty cool, right? Now, let's delete the two divs above and below the `img` tags so you just have `<img src="http://placehold.it/1000x250">`, and then in your `foundation-book.css` file add the following code:

```
img {
  width: 100%;
}
```

Now, go to your browser, refresh it, and see what happens. You will now find that your header is 100 percent of the browser screen and when you resize the window again, Foundation handles the resize for you. Let's keep it like this and move on to the next `<nav>` element.

Since we covered breadcrumbs, we shall now give them a try as shown in the next header. So, after your placeholder image tag, let's insert the following code:

```
<nav class="breadcrumbs">
  <a href="#">Home</a>
  <a href="#" class="unavailable">Nav 1</a>
  <a href="#">Nav 1.2</a>
  <a href="#" class="current">Nav 1.2.1</a>
</nav>
```

You will notice that the breadcrumbs span the entire width of the browser window, which is something we do not want; so, let's modify the code to put them back into our grid, as shown in the following diagram:

```
┌──────────────────────────────────────────────────────────┐
│ Browser Window                                           │
│ ┌──────────────────────────────────────────────────────┐ │
│ │ Nav Bar                                              │ │
│ │                                                      │ │
│ ├──────────────────────────────────────────────────────┤ │
│ │ ┌──────────────────────────────────────────────────┐ │ │
│ │ │   Breadcrumbs                                    │ │ │
│ │ ├──────────────────────────────────────────────────┤ │ │
│ │ │                                                  │ │ │
│ │ │                                                  │ │ │
│ │ │                                                  │ │ │
│ │ │                                                  │ │ │
│ │ │                                                  │ │ │
│ │ │                                                  │ │ │
│ │ │                                                  │ │ │
│ │ │                                                  │ │ │
│ │ └──────────────────────────────────────────────────┘ │ │
│ └──────────────────────────────────────────────────────┘ │
└──────────────────────────────────────────────────────────┘
```

Add the following code:

```
<div class="row">
    <div class="small-12 medium-12 large-12">
      <nav class="breadcrumbs">
        <a href="#">Home</a>
        <a href="#" class="unavailable">Nav 1</a>
        <a href="#">Nav 1.2</a>
        <a href="#" class="current">Nav 1.2.1</a>
      </nav>
    </div>
  </div>
```

It will now look like what is shown in the following screenshot:

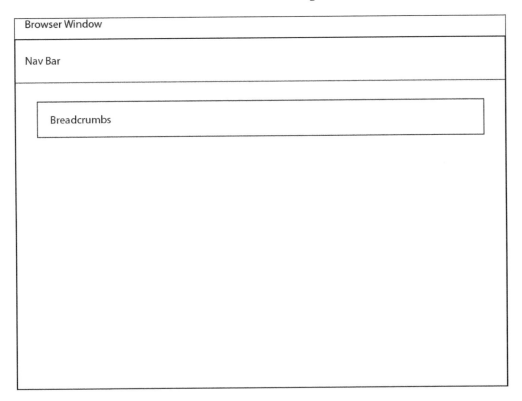

And then in `foundation-book.css`, add the following code:

```
.breadcrumbs {
  margin: 20px 0;
}
```

This will give our breadcrumbs a little breathing room.

Now, let's add some side navigation in our sidebar. Delete the `<p>` tag with the word `"sidebar"` in it and add the following code:

```
<ul class="side-nav">
  <li class="active"><a href="#">Side Nav 1</a></li>
  <li class="divider"></li>
  <li><a href="#">Side Nav 2</a></li>
</ul>
```

You will now have two sidebar elements with a horizontal dividing line between them. If you resize your window so that it's small enough, you will see that on a large and medium screen your sidebar will be on the left, but on a small screen those links will show up below the main content that was to the right on the medium and large screens.

Next, let's try subnavigation or filter navigation. So, right before the `<p>` tag, which contains `"Paragraph of content"`, let's add the following code:

```
<dl class="sub-nav">
  <dt>Sort By:</dt>
  <dd><a href="#">Newest</a></dd>
  <dd><a href="#">Unread</a></dd>
  <dd class="active"><a href="#">Oldest</a></dd>
  <dd><a href="#">Last</a></dd>
</dl>
```

You will see that you have a nice `"Sort By"` `<nav>` element and that `"Oldest"` is active.

Now, let's add in that pagination block of code. So, after the `<p>` tag that contains `"Paragraph of content"`, let's add the following code:

```
<div class="pagination-centered">
  <ul class="pagination">
    <li class="arrow unavailable"><a href="">&laquo;</a></li>
    <li class="current"><a href="">1</a></li>
    <li><a href="">2</a></li>
    <li class="unavailable"><a href="">&hellip;</a></li>
    <li><a href="">9</a></li>
    <li><a href="">10</a></li>
    <li class="arrow"><a href="">&raquo;</a></li>
  </ul>
</div>
```

Refresh your browser and you will see a centered pagination. If you want to left align that pagination in the div, remove `"-centered"` and you can remove the div as well. We will leave it centered, but just know that you can align it to the left if you like.

Our one-page site is starting to come together! There are a couple of other super cool navigation components that Foundation comes with, but we will cover those in *Chapter 5, JavaScript,* and we will build a couple of mini projects that are outside of our one-page website.

Summary

In this chapter, we covered the following points:

- How to use the Foundation navigation system
- How to take that navigation system and make it complex with dropdowns, right-aligned elements, and how to make that same menu work on a small screen
- Learned about and executed breadcrumbs, side navigation, subnavigation, and finally pagination

In the next chapter, we will be talking about all the different elements that Foundation has to offer, from buttons to videos.

4
Elements

One of the most important things about any framework is the elements that you use to customize your projects. Foundation has pretty much any kind of element that you will need. You can easily customize and combine these element types to make well-customized layouts and designs. We will cover the following topics:

- Typography
- Lists
- Blockquote
- V-cards
- Buttons
- Panels
- Pricing tables
- Tables
- Video
- Progress bars
- Keystrokes
- Labels

First, let's get rid of the black border around the columns in our demo site. So, in your `foundation-book.css` script, let's delete the following:

```css
.columns {
    border: 1px solid black;
}
```

Refresh our browser, and you will see that the black border lines are gone. We are going to add a bunch of elements into our one-page website. We will remove them later and get back to building a nice starter site, but we need to try out a bunch of things before we start to make things look pretty. Now, let's get started with some typography.

Typography

Here are the basic styling of the heading elements:

```
<h1>H1</h1>
<h2>H2</h2>
<h3>H3</h3>
<h4>H4</h4>
<h5>H5</h5>
<h6>H6</h6>
```

Let's put them in our code to see what they look like. Under `Sort By:` and code below this image tag, let's add the six header tags. This should be around line 82 in our `index.html` file. Remember, you can always view my code at https://codio.com/kevinhorek/Learning-Zurb-Foundation/ or https://github.com/kevinhorek/Learning-Zurb-Foundation. Refresh your browser, and you will see the six headers.

Subheadings

Perfect! Now that we have the headers in, we can remove them second to sixth headers and just keep `<h1>`. Let's change the text in `<h1>` to `<h1>Welcome</h1>`. Refresh your browser. You also have the ability to use a `subheader` class on any of the header tags, so let's create another `<h1>` tag right below the first one, with the content `To Learning Zurb Foundation`. The tag should look like the following:

```
<h1 class="subheader">To Learning Zurb Foundation</h1>
```

You will see that the only difference is the color of this subheader, which is a shade of gray instead of the almost black color of the regular `<h1>` tag. The gray color is a Foundation default; we will cover how to theme elements later in the book.

You would likely not want to use two `<h1>` tags in a row, especially for SEO (http://accessibility.psu.edu/headings), so let's change this `subheader` class to an `<h2>` tag like this:

```
<h2 class="subheader">To Learning Zurb Foundation</h2>
```

You will see that the text is still gray and the font size is a little smaller as it is a smaller header. This also allows you to format the same heading levels in different ways for different sections.

The small tag

Next, let's add in the ability to format a part of the text in the header tags in a manner that is different from the rest of the header. If we add a small tag inside the header tag and then put our name in it followed by a comma, we will see that the font is formatted differently from the rest of the heading. So, let's try this. Type in your name instead of Kevin:

```
<h1>Welcome <small>Kevin,</small></h1>
```

This looks funny from a design perspective, but you can see that the small tag makes the text a lot smaller than the <h1> tag and even smaller than the subheader class that is used with our <h2> tag. You can use CSS to change the formatting of how your small tag renders inside your <h1> tags. So, let's give this a shot. In our foundation-book.css file, after our breadcrumbs class, on line 10, let's add the following:

```
h1 small {
    font-size: 2.75rem;
    color: #008cba;
}
```

The color is the default Foundation blue, so you can see that we made the small text the same size as the rest of the text in the <h1> tag and made it blue.

Lists

Next, let's cover lists. These are pretty standard, but you can write whatever custom CSS you want to customize lists for your projects. However, there are a few things you should know that can help with these customizations. So, let's start with the basic list. Enter the following code below your paragraph of content; this should be around line 76 and make sure it is above your pagination:

```
<ul>
    <li>List 1</li>
    <li>List 2</li>
    <li>List 3</li>
</ul>
```

You will see your basic list with disk bullets. You can include any of these classes in `<ul>`: circle, square, disk, or no-bullet. Give it a try! For our one-page demo site, we will use the square bullet, as shown in the following code:

```
<ul class="square">
  <li>List 1</li>
  <li>List 2</li>
  <li>List 3</li>
</ul>
```

Inline lists

If you want your list items to not have bullets and be inline, you can just use the inline-list class. This is really useful for menus, filters, and breadcrumbs. The code would be as follows:

```
<ul class="inline-list">
  <li>List 1</li>
  <li>List 2</li>
  <li>List 3</li>
</ul>
```

This will list the elements as follows:

```
List 1     List 2     List 3
```

Go ahead and give this a try and then change the class back.

You also have the ability to nest lists inside each other. So, let's give this a try by modifying our `<li>` tag for List 2 to the following:

```
<ul class="square">
  <li>List 1</li>
  <li>List 2
    <ul>
      <li>List 2.1</li>
      <li>List 2.2</li>
      <li>List 2.3</li>
    </ul>
  </li>
  <li>List 3</li>
</ul>
```

Now, say we want to indent our list to the left. Let's go to our `foundation-book.css` file and on line 10 add the following:

```
ul.square {
margin-left: 4em;
}
```

You will now see your list indented. If you want to give your list a class other than `square`, replace `square` with whatever class name you want.

Definition lists

Next, let's cover definition lists. Foundation formats them a little different from the browser's default format. Let's try them out. On line 88, add the following code:

```
<hr />

<dl>
  <dt>Title</dt>
  <dd>Content would go here</dd>
</dl>

<hr />
```

The `hr` tags are not needed for the definition list, but we should see what `hr` tags look like. These tags will separate our definition list from the unordered list above and the pagination below.

Ordered lists work in the same way that they work outside Foundation, so we are not going to cover them in this book.

Blockquote

Now, let's cover blockquote. Foundation does a nice job of handling blockquotes. Let's try them out by inserting this code on or around line 97; type in your name instead of my name:

```
<blockquote>Learning Zurb Foundation
  <cite>Kevin Horek</cite>
</blockquote>
```

V-cards

Next, let's cover v-cards. For those of you who do not know what a v-card is, it is basically an electronic business card. You put your name and contact information on them, just like you would on a regular business card. Let's go ahead and create one. You can insert your information instead of mine, but insert this code on our side menu on or around line 127; this will go under your unordered list with `Side Nav 1` and `Side Nav 2`:

```
<ul class="vcard">
  <li class="fn">Kevin Horek</li>
  <li class="street-address">My Street</li>
  <li class="locality">My City</li>
  <li><span class="state">My State</span>, <span class="zip">90210</span></li>
  <li class="email"><a href="mailto:kevin@kevinhorek.com">kevin@kevinhorek.com</a></li>
</ul>
```

For more information on v-cards and which classes you can use, visit `http://en.wikipedia.org/wiki/VCard`.

Buttons

One thing Foundation does really well, is buttons. We are about to cover all the options you have with buttons. So, let's get started.

You can turn any `<a>` or `<button>` tag into a Foundation button by adding the `button` class. So, on or around line 135, on your left-hand side column and under `vcard`, let's add the following:

```
<a href="#" class="button">Button</a>
```

You will see a simple blue button. You also have the ability to set a few sizes for the button. You need to keep the `button` class, but you can put another class such as `tiny`, `small`, `medium`, `large`, and `expand` in the code. Let's try this out by adding a `large` class to our button:

```
<a href="#" class="button large">Button</a>
```

You will see that the button gets larger; try others. When you try to expand the button, it will take up the entire width of the column that it is in.

The next thing you might want to do is add rounded corners to our button, so go ahead and add the `radius` class and then try adding `round` to our button:

```
<a href="#" class="button large radius">Button</a>
and  <a href="#" class="button round">Button</a>
```

You will notice that you can have multiple classes on your button to make Foundation style your button differently. Try playing with the combinations and see what you like.

You can also change the color of your button by adding a second, third, or fourth class named `secondary`, `success`, `alert`, or even `disabled`. We will cover how to add even more colors to the button later, but for now, let's add the `success` class to our button to make it green, as shown in the following code:

```
<a href="#" class="button large radius success">Button</a>
```

Drop-down buttons

Now that we have a button, what if we want to make that button a dropdown? Well, we can easily do this by adding `data-dropdown="dropdown"` to our `<a>` tag and then the `dropdown` class. Then, we need to create an unordered list and give that an `id` value with the same name that we put in `data-dropdown`, which in this case is just `"dropdown"`. We then need to add `"data-dropdown-content"` to the `<ul>` tag and a `f-dropdown` class. Go ahead and add the following code on or around line 137:

```
<a href="#" data-dropdown="dropdown" class="medium round button
dropdown">Button with a dropdown</a>
<ul id="dropdown" data-dropdown-content class="f-dropdown">
  <li><a href="#">Dropdown Link 1</a></li>
  <li><a href="#">Dropdown Link 2</a></li>
</ul>
```

Pretty cool, right? You will also notice that you can use any of the button customizations such as `tiny`, `small`, `medium`, `large`, `secondary`, `success`, `alert`, `disabled`, `rounded`, and `radius` on these buttons. Also, try removing all the classes on your button's link tag; you will notice that you lose all the button styles and you just have a link on which once you click, you get a dropdown of that link. You can also control the width of your drop-down menu and can apply the following classes on your `<ul>` element before or after the `f-dropdown` class:

- `tiny`: This class gives the drop-down menu of a maximum width of 200 px
- `small`: This class gives the drop-down menu of a maximum width of 300 px

- medium: This class gives the drop-down menu of a maximum width of 500 px
- large: This class gives the drop-down menu of a maximum width of 800 px

Give these a shot on your drop-down menu; let's add the tiny class to ours, as shown in the following code:

```
<a href="#" data-dropdown="dropdown" class="medium round button
dropdown">Button with a dropdown</a>
<ul id="drop" data-dropdown-content class="f-dropdown tiny">
  <li><a href="#">Dropdown Link 1</a></li>
  <li><a href="#">Dropdown Link 2</a></li>
</ul>
```

You will see that drop-down menu is set as max-width equal to 200px.

Drop-down buttons with images and text

Great! We have a button with a drop-down menu on links, but what if you want to have some text and an image in these button dropdowns? Well, Foundation allows you to do this. On or around line 143, let's add the following:

```
<a href="#" data-dropdown="dropdowncontent" class="medium round button
dropdown">Button with a content dropdown</a>
<div id="dropdowncontent" data-dropdown-content class="f-dropdown
content">
  <p>Here is some text</p>
  <p>Here is an image</p>
  <img src="http://placehold.it/300x250">
</div>
```

Just like before, we need to give data-dropdown a unique name and make sure that this is the same ID we use on our content div. Perfect! We now have the ability to create some well-customized buttons with clickable dropdowns. What if you want to make the dropdown appear when you hover instead of click? Well, all you need to do is add data-option; you do this by adding data-options="is_hover:true" to our <a> tag, as shown in the following code:

```
<a href="#" data-dropdown="dropdowncontent" class="medium round
button dropdown" data-options="is_hover:true">Button with a content
dropdown</a>
<div id="dropdowncontent" data-dropdown-content class="f-dropdown
content">
  <p>Here is some text</p>
  <p>Here is an image</p>
  <img src="http://placehold.it/300x250">
</div>
```

You very rarely need to use a `hover` state on the modern Web; `hover` states do not work on tablets or phones. Remember, any of these examples will work if you remove all the `button` classes from your `<a>` tags and turn them into text links.

Split drop-down buttons

There is one more type of drop-down button and it is called the split drop-down button. It allows you to split your button up into a button and a drop-down menu. Let's try it out by adding the following code on or around line 150:

```
<a href="#" class="button secondary split">Button Split <span data-dropdown="dropsplit"></span></a><br>
<ul id="dropsplit" class="f-dropdown" data-dropdown-content>
  <li><a href="#">Dropdown Link 1</a></li>
  <li><a href="#">Dropdown Link 2</a></li>
</ul>
```

You can see that it looks pretty similar to the buttons we just covered, but the only part that is different and creates the dropdown is the `split` part on the right-hand side of the button. You will also notice that the button is now of gray color. This is because of the `secondary` class on the `<a>` tag. You can also apply the `size` classes as well as `round` and `radius`.

Button groups

By now, you must be thinking there is a lot you can do with a simple button, but what if I want to group my buttons together to make a group of buttons? Well, like everything else in Foundation, this is very easy to do, so let's move back to our main content area and on or around line 159, you will see the following:

```
<div class="row">
    <div class="large-2 columns">2 Columns</div>
    <div class="large-8 large-offset-2 columns">8 Columns, Offset by 2 Columns</div>
  </div>
```

Let's modify it to be:

```
<div class="row">
  <div class="large-2 columns">2 Columns</div>
  <div class="large-8 large-offset-2 columns">

    <ul class="button-group radius">
```

```
        <li><a href="#" class="button secondary">Button 1</a></li>
        <li><a href="#" class="button secondary">Button 2</a></li>
        <li><a href="#" class="button secondary">Button 3</a></li>
    </ul>

    </div>
  </div>
```

We are getting rid of the 8 Columns, Offset by 2 Columns text inside the div with the large-8 large-offset-2 columns class and adding in our button group. You will notice our button group is now inside the Foundation grid, but there is no margin and it is right up against the text and the bottom of the browser. We will be doing more theming later on in this book, but let's make it look a little better for now. So, go to foundation-book.css and on or around line 19, add the following:

```css
.button-group {
  margin: 40px 0px;
}
```

This will give the top and bottom of the button group some margin. Now, let's copy and paste this button group under itself and wrap both of the button groups in a div with the button-bar class. A button bar is a group of two button groups. We also want to add them on their own line, but inside the Foundation grid. So, let's also wrap everything in a div with the large-12 columns class and wrap that div with a div with the row class. The code will look as follows:

```html
<div class="row">
    <div class="large-12 columns">

    <div class="button-bar">

      <ul class="button-group radius">
        <li><a href="#" class="button secondary">Button 1</a></li>
        <li><a href="#" class="button secondary">Button 2</a></li>
        <li><a href="#" class="button secondary">Button 3</a></li>
      </ul>

      <ul class="button-group radius">
        <li><a href="#" class="button secondary">Button 1</a></li>
        <li><a href="#" class="button secondary">Button 2</a></li>
        <li><a href="#" class="button secondary">Button 3</a></li>
      </ul>

    </div>

    </div>
  </div>
```

You will see that you have two groups of three buttons side by side. This is great for toolbars in your projects or groups of navigation elements.

You can do a lot with buttons, so make sure you try out combinations of what we talked about, and we will cover how to style buttons even further in an upcoming chapter.

Panels

Panels are basically elements with a background and a border. By default, panels give you a gray background and a dark gray border. So, let's give them a shot. On or around line 191, add the following:

```
<div class="panel">
    <p>
      This is some default panel content.
    </p>
  </div>
```

You will see that the panel takes up the entire 12 columns, so let's change this and make it take up only 6 columns and add a second panel that takes up the other 6 columns. So, let's change our code to:

```
<div class="small-12 large-6 columns">

<div class="panel">
   <p>
     This is some default panel content.
   </p>
   </div>

</div>

<div class="small-12 large-6 columns">

 <div class="panel">
    <p>
      This is some default panel content.
    </p>
    </div>

</div>
```

You will notice that now as we nested the 6 columns inside the 12 columns, you get two panels side by side in these 6 columns, but you also get a gutter on either side of the panels. They also do not take up the entire width of the row. You might or might not want this effect, but let's keep this anyway. Let's create a new row and add the same panel code into this new row and see what happens. So, on or around line 214, let's add:

```
<div class="row">

  <div class="small-12 large-6 columns">

    <div class="panel">
    <p>
      This is some default panel content.
    </p>
    </div>

  </div>

  <div class="small-12 large-6 columns">

    <div class="panel">
    <p>
      This is some default panel content.
    </p>
    </div>

  </div>

</div>
```

Now, you will get the same two panels side by side, but they will take up the full width of the row. As you get more and more comfortable with Foundation, you will learn these types of tricks, and we will cover the ones that have been useful to me.

You can also add a couple of additional classes to panels. If you want to round the corners, you can use the radius class and you can add the callout class. The callout class will make your panel blue; you can change this with CSS or Sass once we cover them later in the book. So, let's add both of these classes to our second panel in the new row that we just created. Your code should now look like this:

```
<div class="row">

  <div class="small-12 large-6 columns">
```

```
<div class="panel">
<p>
  This is some default panel content.
</p>
</div>

</div>

<div class="small-12 large-6 columns">

<div class="panel callout radius">
<p>
  This is some default panel content.
</p>
</div>

</div>

</div>
```

You will now see a blue panel with some rounded corners. Now, let's duplicate the `<p>` tag in the second blue panel. Your code should look like this now:

```
<div class="panel callout radius">
  <p>
    This is some default panel content.
  </p>
  <p>
    This is some default panel content.
  </p>
</div>
```

You will notice that now the height of this panel, due to the additional content, has been increased and that it does not vertically line up. This might be what you want, but in a lot of cases, you would want it to line up, so let's fix this. Add `data-equalizer` to the `<div>` row and `data-equalizer-watch` to the panel divs, as shown in the following code:

```
<div class="row" data-equalizer>

  <div class="small-12 large-6 columns">

    <div class="panel" data-equalizer-watch>
    <p>
```

```
      This is some default panel content.
    </p>
    </div>

  </div>

  <div class="small-12 large-6 columns">

    <div class="panel callout radius" data-equalizer-watch>
    <p>
      This is some default panel content.
    </p>
    <p>
      This is some default panel content.
    </p>
    </div>

  </div>

</div>
```

Like magic or a little JavaScript, the two panels are now of the same height. JavaScript calculates the height of the longest panel and sets the others to the same height.

Pricing tables

If you are using Foundation for your startup, you might want to have pricing and lay this pricing out in a nice, easy-to-read list. Foundation comes with a nice default template. So, let's try it out. On or around line 241, let's insert the following code:

```
<ul class="pricing-table">
  <li class="title">Title Of Pricing</li>
  <li class="price">$19.95</li>
  <li class="description">Pricing description</li>
  <li class="bullet-item">What's Included 1</li>
  <li class="bullet-item">What's Included 1</li>
  <li class="bullet-item">What's Included 1</li>
  <li class="cta-button"><a class="button" href="#">Select</a></li>
</ul>
```

Pricing tables in columns

You will notice that a pricing table takes up the entire width of the screen. You might not want this, so let's add in a second one and put them both inside the Foundation grid. Let's give this code a shot:

```
<div class="row">
  <div class="small-12 medium-6 large-6 columns">
    <ul class="pricing-table">
      <li class="title">Title Of Pricing</li>
      <li class="price">$19.95</li>
      <li class="description">Pricing description</li>
      <li class="bullet-item">What's Included 1</li>
      <li class="bullet-item">What's Included 1</li>
      <li class="bullet-item">What's Included 1</li>
      <li class="cta-button"><a class="button" href="#">Select</a></li>
    </ul>
  </div>
  <div class="small-12 medium-6 large-6 columns">
    <ul class="pricing-table">
      <li class="title">Title Of Pricing</li>
      <li class="price">$19.95</li>
      <li class="description">Pricing description</li>
      <li class="bullet-item">What's Included 1</li>
      <li class="bullet-item">What's Included 1</li>
      <li class="bullet-item">What's Included 1</li>
      <li class="cta-button"><a class="button" href="#">Select</a></li>
    </ul>
  </div>
</div>
```

Pricing tables in columns without a gutter

Great! We have a pricing table. This looks alright, but what if you want the pricing tables right next to each other, on a desktop and a tablet. Let's duplicate our pricing row and modify the code to look like this:

```
<div class="row">

  <ul class="pricing-table small-11 small-centered medium-6 medium-
uncentered medium-6 large-6 columns">
    <li class="title">Title Of Pricing</li>
```

```
        <li class="price">$19.95</li>
        <li class="description">Pricing description</li>
        <li class="bullet-item">What's Included 1</li>
        <li class="bullet-item">What's Included 1</li>
        <li class="bullet-item">What's Included 1</li>
        <li class="cta-button"><a class="button" href="#">Select</a></li>
    </ul>
    <ul class="pricing-table small-11 small-centered medium-6 medium-
uncentered medium-6 large-6 columns">
        <li class="title">Title Of Pricing</li>
        <li class="price">$19.95</li>
        <li class="description">Pricing description</li>
        <li class="bullet-item">What's Included 1</li>
        <li class="bullet-item">What's Included 1</li>
        <li class="bullet-item">What's Included 1</li>
        <li class="cta-button"><a class="button" href="#">Select</a></li>
    </ul>

</div>
```

Fixing border issues

Awesome! However, you will notice that the backgrounds do not go to the edge of the borders. Let's use a little CSS to fix this. Go to your `foundation-book.css` file and remove the left and right padding on the `column` class for the pricing table. Here is the code:

```
.pricing-table.columns {
  padding-left: 0;
  padding-right: 0;
}
```

Nice. Looks great! Notice that we set the small grid size to 11 and then centered the grid, so you get some padding back on either side on a small screen. If you do not want this padding and you want the pricing tables to touch the edge of the screen, remove `small-centered` and `medium-uncentered` and change `small-11` to `small-12`. Here is what the code should look like:

```
<div class="row">

    <ul class="pricing-table small-12 medium-6 large-6 columns">
      <li class="title">Title Of Pricing</li>
      <li class="price">$19.95</li>
      <li class="description">Pricing description</li>
```

```
          <li class="bullet-item">What's Included 1</li>
          <li class="bullet-item">What's Included 1</li>
          <li class="bullet-item">What's Included 1</li>
          <li class="cta-button"><a class="button" href="#">Select</a></
li>
      </ul>
      <ul class="pricing-table small-12 medium-6 large-6 columns">
          <li class="title">Title Of Pricing</li>
          <li class="price">$19.95</li>
          <li class="description">Pricing description</li>
          <li class="bullet-item">What's Included 1</li>
          <li class="bullet-item">What's Included 1</li>
          <li class="bullet-item">What's Included 1</li>
          <li class="cta-button"><a class="button" href="#">Select</a></
li>
      </ul>

  </div>
```

Tables

Tables are frowned upon, but sometimes you absolutely need to use them in rare situations. Foundation has a default styling for tables. Let's give it a try. On or around line 289, let's insert the following code:

```
<div class="row">
  <table>
    <thead>
      <tr>
        <th>Header</th>
        <th>Header</th>
      </tr>
    </thead>
    <tbody>
      <tr>
        <td>Col 1</td>
        <td>Col 2</td>
      </tr>
      <tr>
        <td>Col 1</td>
        <td>Col 2</td>
      </tr>
    </tbody>
  </table>
</div>
```

You will notice that we are just putting the table in a `row` div to contain the table to our grid, but not worrying about specifying how many columns it will use at different screen sizes. This is because our table is small and tables work terribly on a small screen. Zurb has created a responsive tables add-on that is not part of Foundation, but if you are interested, you can read more about this at `http://zurb.com/playground/responsive-tables`.

Video

You are likely to add video to one of your projects, so let's make this responsive. So, here is how you add video. On or around line 309, inside our last row div, but after the table, let's add the following:

```
<div class="flex-video">
        <iframe width="420" height="315" src="https://www.youtube.
com/watch?v=8FfAGiUiOWk&list=TLuNeo0ehMwmKsLJj2bu5yD0qPMtPN8D0Q"
frameborder="0" allowfullscreen></iframe>
</div>
```

If your video is widescreen and/or vimeo, just add a `widescreen` class and/or `vimeo`, like this:

```
<div class="flex-video widescreen vimeo">
        <iframe width="420" height="315" src="https://www.youtube.
com/watch?v=8FfAGiUiOWk&list=TLuNeo0ehMwmKsLJj2bu5yD0qPMtPN8D0Q"
frameborder="0" allowfullscreen></iframe>
</div>
```

You can put the video inside the grid as well, and it will act like any other element and resize properly for the screen.

Progress bars

Foundation also comes with progress bars. Let's try them out and put them inside the same div as the table and video. On or around line 313, let's insert this code:

```
<div class="progress">
        <span class="meter"></span>
</div>
```

It looks fancy, doesn't it? We have a blue progress bar that is 100 percent complete. If you want to try and see the progress bar, say 60 percent complete, you can add a `style` tag to your span and set it to a 60 percent width, as shown in the following code:

```
<div class="progress">
        <span class="meter" style="width: 60%"></span>
</div>
```

Like a lot of Foundation elements, you can add `secondary`, `alert`, `success`, `radius`, and `round` after `progress`. Go ahead and try them out.

Keystrokes

If you want to showcase keystrokes, you can use the `<kbd>` tag around the key you want. An example of this is `<kbd>F</kbd>`.

Label

If you want little callouts in your content, you can use a label. These are just little elements that have a colored background and text inside. Go ahead and try it out.

```
<span class="label">I am a label</span>
```

Again, you can add the `secondary`, `alert`, `success`, `radius`, and `round` elements after `progress`.

Print styles

You have the ability to turn things on and off for print. You can use the `show-for-print` or `hide-for-print` class in your code. You can try these out on a few elements if you want and view the print preview.

Sliders

Foundation also allows you to have horizontal and vertical sliders. So, let's add one right below our `progress-bar` div; this will be around or on line 317:

```
<div class="range-slider" data-slider>
<span class="range-slider-handle"></span>
<span class="range-slider-active-segment"></span>
  <input type="hidden">
</div>
```

Go to your browser and refresh, and you will see that you now have a slider. Pretty cool, right? So, let's do some customizations to this slider. Right after the `range-slider` class, add `radius`, `round`, or `disabled` and depending on what you pick, you will get one of the three stylings on the slider. For this example, we will use `round`. So, add it as shown in the following code:

```
<div class="range-slider round" data-slider>
<span class="range-slider-handle"></span>
<span class="range-slider-active-segment"></span>
  <input type="hidden">
</div>
```

Horizontal sliders are useful, but let's turn this into a vertical slider with just a bit more code. After the `round` class, add `vertical-range` and after `data-slider`, add `data-options="vertical: true;"`. The code should look like this:

```
<div class="range-slider round vertical-range" data-slider data-slider
data-options="vertical: true;">
  <span class="range-slider-handle"></span>
  <span class="range-slider-active-segment"></span>
  <input type="hidden">
</div>
```

Go ahead and refresh your browser, and you will see that you now have a vertical slider. Pretty cool. Now you might be thinking that having a slider is great, but it would be nice to have a number value that changes when you slide the slider. This requires a bit more of code, so we will create a new slider by adding this below our current vertical slider. This code should go on or around line 321:

```
<div class="row">
<div class="large-6 columns">
    <div class="range-slider" data-slider data-options="display_
selector: #sliderOutput1;">
      <span class="range-slider-handle"></span>
      <span class="range-slider-active-segment"></span>
    </div>
  </div>
  <div class="large-1 end columns">
    <span id="sliderOutput1"></span>
  </div>
</div>
```

Go ahead and refresh your browser. You will see that you now have a horizontal slider with a number value that changes as you slide the slider. This will also work on a vertical slider. You will notice that your slider goes up and down by one number. You might want this or you might want to jump by a set number of steps. So, let's add a little more code. So, every time you drag the slider, the value moves by 10 instead of 1. To do this, we just add step: 10; after #sliderOutput1 in data-options. So, let's give that a shot:

```
<div class="row">
    <div class="large-6 columns">
    <div class="range-slider" data-slider data-options="display_
selector: #sliderOutput1; step: 10;">
        <span class="range-slider-handle"></span>
        <span class="range-slider-active-segment"></span>
    </div>
    </div>
    <div class="large-1 end columns">
    <span id="sliderOutput1"></span>
    </div>
</div>
```

You will notice that the slider now moves by a value of 10 when you move the slider. The last thing that you can do with sliders is set a default range of numbers. You might want the steps to go from 10 to 50, so let's try that by adding after step: 10; start: 10; end: 50;. The code should look like this:

```
<div class="row">
  <div class="large-6 columns">
    <div class="range-slider" data-slider data-options="display_
selector: #sliderOutput1; step: 10; start: 10; end: 50;">
        <span class="range-slider-handle"></span>
        <span class="range-slider-active-segment"></span>
    </div>
  </div>
  <div class="large-1 end columns">
    <span id="sliderOutput1"></span>
  </div>
</div>
```

There you have it. You can now build some well-customized sliders with Foundation.

Alerts

If you are using Foundation with any sort of content management system or web app, you will need to alert the user when different things happen. Alerts are usually just colored bars that are themed based on the type of notification. Let's add the default one below our sliders. So, on or around line 335, let's add:

```
<div data-alert class="alert-box">
Hello, I am an alert box!
  <a href="#" class="close">&times;</a>
</div>
```

Go ahead and refresh your browser. You will see a blue alert box with the text **Hello, I am an alert box!**. You will also notice an **x**. If you click on this **x**, the alert will fade out. Just like in most Foundation elements, you have the ability to theme your alerts by just adding some classes after the `alert-box` class. You can add `success`, `warning`, `info`, `alert`, `secondary` as well as `radius` and `round`. Let's try a couple of these together. Go ahead and add `success` and `round` to our alert box; the code will look like this:

```
<div data-alert class="alert-box success round">
Hello, I am an alert box!
  <a href="#" class="close">&times;</a>
</div>
```

When you refresh your browser, you will see that you now have a green alert box that is round.

Tooltips

Now let's cover tooltips. These are pretty quick to implement. Let's try one by adding the following code above our alert box. This should be on or around line 335:

```
<p><span data-tooltip class="has-tip" title="`Content of
tooltip">Tooltip</span></p>
```

Make sure that you put the tooltip code above the alert and inside a `<p>` tag to give it some space, and when you hover over the text, the tooltip will appear over the alert. If you want to change where the tooltip shows up, you can add a position by adding an extra class to `has-tip`. These classes are: `tip-bottom`, `tip-top`, `tip-left`, and `tip-right`. You can also add a third class: `radius` or `round`. So, let's add a couple of these to our tooltip:

```
<p><span data-tooltip class="has-tip tip-top round" title="`Content of
tooltip">Tooltip</span></p>
```

You can also choose the screen size of the tooltips by adding `data-options="show_on:large"`. So, let's try this, as shown in the following code:

```
<p><span data-tooltip class="has-tip tip-top round" title="Content of
tooltip" data-options="show_on:large">Tooltip</span></p>
```

If you refresh your browser, you will see the tooltip still works when you hover over it. However, if you resize your browser to a medium or small width, you will see that the tooltip stops working. If you want to disable tooltips on a touch screen, you can change `show_on:large` to `disable_for_touch:true`.

Utility

Foundation has a bunch of general classes that you will likely use in many of your projects. The most popular utility classes are as follows:

Class	What it does
right	This class floats an element to the right
left	This class floats an element to the left
text-left	This class aligns text to the left
text-right	This class aligns text to the right
text-center	This class aligns text to the center
text-justify	This class justifies your text
hide	This class hides an element

To use a class like `text-right`, you should use the following code:

```
<p class="text-right">This text will be right aligned</p>
```

For a full list of utility classes, you can visit
`http://foundation.zurb.com/docs/utility-classes.html`.

Visibility

Visibility classes are just as useful and easy to use as utility classes. Here is a table of the most popular ones:

Class	Use
show-for-small-only	This class shows content on small screens only
show-for-medium-up	This class shows content on medium or larger screens
show-for-medium-only	This class shows content on medium-sized screens only
show-for-large-up	This class shows content on large or larger screens
show-for-large-only	This class shows content for large screens only
show-for-xlarge-up	This class shows content for extra large and larger screens
show-for-xlarge-only	This class shows content for extra large screens only
show-for-xxlarge-up	This class shows content for 2X large and larger screens
hide-for-medium-up	This class hides content for medium or larger screens
hide-for-medium-only	This class hides content for medium-sized screens
hide-for-large-up	This class hides content for large or larger screens
hide-for-large-only	This class hides content for large screens
hide-for-xlarge-up	This class hides content for extra large and larger screens
hide-for-xlarge-only	This class hides content for extra large screens
hide-for-xxlarge-up	This class hides content for 2X or larger screens
show-for-touch	This class shows content on a touch device
hide-for-touch	This class hides content on a touch device

The following shows how to implement these in your code. Let's try the show-for-touch class:

```
<p class="show-for-touch">This text will show on a touch device</p>
```

Now, what if we want to show or hide elements for a screen reader. Well, Foundation has the ability to show and hide elements to only screen readers. This really makes Foundation have pretty customizable accessibility options. Here is a table of all the accessibility options you have:

Class	Use
hidden-for-small-only	This class hides elements on small screens only
hidden-for-medium-up	This class hides elements on medium or larger screens
hidden-for-medium-only	This class hides elements on medium-sized screens only
hidden-for-large-up	This class hides elements on large or larger screens
hidden-for-large-only	This class hides elements for large screens only
hidden-for-xlarge-up	This class hides elements for extra large and larger screens
hidden-for-xlarge-only	This class hides elements for extra large screens only
hidden-for-xxlarge-up	This class hides elements for 2X large and larger screens
visible-for-small-only	This class makes elements visible on small screens only
visible-for-medium-up	This class makes elements visible on medium and larger screens
visible-for-medium-only	This class makes elements visible on medium-sized screens only
visible-for-large-up	This class makes elements visible on large and larger screens
visible-for-large-only	This class makes elements visible on large screens only
visible-for-xlarge-up	This class makes elements visible on extra large and larger screens
visible-for-xlarge-only	This class makes elements visible on extra large screens only
visible-for-xxlarge-up	This class makes elements visible on 2X large and larger screens

Switches

Foundation has a switches element. So, let's try this out by setting a couple of switches. After our alert box, on or around line 342, let's add the following two switches:

```
<div class="switch">
  <input id="ourswitch1" type="radio" name="switches" checked>
  <label for="ourswitch1"></label>
</div>
<div class="switch">
  <input id="ourswitch2" type="radio" name="switches">
  <label for="ourswitch2"></label>
</div>
```

You will see that if you click the grayed-out switch, it will deactivate the other one. This can be useful for your projects. You might want to just have one switch to show, say something like on or off, and you can do that as well. Instead of using radio buttons, you will use a checkbox switch. So, let's add the following code below our radio button switches:

```
<div class="switch">
  <input id="switching" type="checkbox">
  <label for="switching"></label>
</div>
```

Just like a lot of Foundation elements, you have the ability to add the radius and round classes, and you can combine these with tiny, small, and large. To use any of these or a combination, you will just add these after the switch class like this:

```
<div class="switch round tiny">
  <input id="switching" type="checkbox">
  <label for="switching"></label>
</div>
```

The icon bar

Similar to a lot of iOS navigation, Foundation has included an icon bar. Let's try this out by adding the following code after our switches on or around line 357:

```
<div class="icon-bar three-up">
  <a class="item">
    <img src="img/arrow.png">
    <label>Arrow One</label>
  </a>
```

```
<a class="item">
  <img src="img/arrow.png">
  <label>Arrow Two</label>
</a>
<a class="item">
  <img src="img/arrow.png">
  <label>Arrow Three</label>
</a>
</div>
```

Refresh your browser and you will see an icon bar. If you need the arrow image, it is in the `img` folder in `Chapter 4` of my Codio project (`https://codio.com/kevinhorek/Learning-Zurb-Foundation/tree/Chapter-4/`). You can use any icon you like. Once you open this folder, right-click on the image and hit **Preview Static**. It will open a new tab and you can save the image. The image is white, so it will look like nothing in that tab.

We have now covered all the Foundation elements. You might be thinking, "What about forms?" We will cover this in *Chapter 5, JavaScript*. You can perform some really cool validation with forms, so we will cover it all together.

Summary

In this chapter, we covered how to use the Foundation elements and how to work with elements to make them responsive. We also learned how we can use different code tweaks to get the elements formatted in a way we want them to be laid out.

In the next chapter, we will be talking about all the different JavaScript libraries that come with Foundation and how to get them working in your project.

5
JavaScript

In this chapter, we will be covering how to use the Foundation JavaScript components. They will add a lot of advanced interactivity to your projects and make your projects shine. We will cover the following topics:

- Magellan sticky navigation
- Off-canvas navigation
- Interchange responsive content
- Orbit slider
- Clearing
- Forms
- Form validation
- Reveal
- Joyride
- Accordion
- Tabs

Before we get into the JavaScript, make sure you copy your code folder from *Chapter 4, Elements*, and make a folder in *Chapter 5, JavaScript*. Let's delete a bunch of elements so we can start with a cleaner file, but you will likely want the work we did in *Chapter 4, Elements*, for reference later on in this book when we add some of those elements back in or when you use Foundation in your projects after this book.

So let's delete the code following this image tag on or around line 47:

```
<img src="http://placehold.it/1000x250">
```

Then stop before the following line of code:

```
<script src="js/vendor/jquery.js"></script>
```

Thus, your `index.html` file should look like the following code snippet:

```html
<!doctype html>
<html class="no-js" lang="en">

<head>
    <meta charset="utf-8" />
    <meta name="viewport" content="width=device-width, initial-
scale=1.0" />
    <title>Learning Zurb Foundation</title>
    <link rel="stylesheet" href="css/foundation.css" />
  <link rel="stylesheet" href="css/foundation-book.css" />
  <script src="js/vendor/modernizr.js"></script>
</head>

<body>

<nav class="top-bar" data-topbar>
    <ul class="title-area">
      <li class="name">
        <h1><a href="#">Logo</a></h1>
      </li>
      <li class="toggle-topbar menu-icon"><a href="#"><span>Nav</
span></a></li>
    </ul>

    <section class="top-bar-section">
      <ul class="left">
        <li class="active"><a href="#">Nav 1</a></li>
        <li class="has-dropdown">
        <a href="#">Nav 2</a>
      <ul class="dropdown">
        <li><a href="#">Nav 2.1</a></li>
        <li><a href="#">Nav 2.2</a></li>
        <li><a href="#">Nav 2.3</a></li>
        <li><a href="#">Nav 2.4</a></li>
```

```
        </ul>
      </li>
      <li><a href="#">Nav 3</a></li>
      <li><a href="#">Nav 4</a></li>
      <li><a href="#">Nav 5</a></li>
    </ul>

    <ul class="right">
      <li><a href="#">Nav 6</a></li>
      <li><a href="#">Nav 7</a></li>
    </ul>

  </section>
</nav>

  <img src="http://placehold.it/1000x250">

  <script src="js/vendor/jquery.js"></script>
  <script src="js/foundation.min.js"></script>
  <script>
    $(document).foundation();
  </script>
  </body>
</html>
```

Magellan sticky navigation

Let's start off with something that is quite popular and can make your site ride the navigation trends of the Web. This type of navigation is called sticky navigation; in Foundation they call this component Magellan Sticky Nav. This type of navigation is when you have a navigation bar below some elements on your site and when you vertically scroll past this menu the menu sticks to the top of the screen and stays with you until you get to the bottom of the page. If you scroll back up past where the sticky nav was, it will unstick and sit back on the page. Do not worry if this does not quite make sense yet, we will be trying this together in a second. Remember you can follow along with me at https://codio.com/kevinhorek/Learning-Zurb-Foundation/ or on GitHub at https://github.com/kevinhorek.

On or around line 49, let's add the following code:

```
<div class="row">
  <div class="small-12 medium-12 large-12 columns">
  <div data-magellan-expedition="fixed">
    <dl class="sub-nav">
    <dd data-magellan-arrival="navone">
      <a href="#navone">Nav One</a>
    </dd>
    <dd data-magellan-arrival="navtwo">
      <a href="#navtwo">Nav Two</a>
    </dd>
    <dd data-magellan-arrival="navthree">
      <a href="#navthree">Nav Three</a>
    </dd>
    <dd data-magellan-arrival="navfour">
      <a href="#navfour">Nav Four</a>
    </dd>
    </dl>
    </div>
    </div>
</div>
```

Then on or around line 68, after the div with `data-magellan-expedition="fixed"`, let's add the following code; you can use whatever text you want in the paragraph. I got my lorem ipsum from `http://www.lipsum.com`:

```
<a name="navone"></a>
  <h3 data-magellan-destination="navone">Nav One</h3>

  <p>
    Lorem ipsum dolor sit amet, consectetur adipiscing elit.
    Suspendisse ac ultrices justo. Integer sed ligula euismod,
    consequat ante sit amet, consequat mauris. Quisque vehicula
    est pulvinar tristique rhoncus. Ut mollis tincidunt nisl, non
    mattis diam congue a. Integer sed tortor felis. Etiam vel
    condimentum lacus, vitae adipiscing lacus. Duis consequat diam
    a varius tristique. Pellentesque tempor leo posuere, lacinia
    metus nec, faucibus risus. Aliquam nunc lacus, malesuada et
    elementum sed, feugiat in turpis. Etiam a purus ligula.
    Curabitur vel magna lectus.
  </p>

  <a name="navtwo"></a>
  <h3 data-magellan-destination="navtwo">Nav Two</h3>
```

```
<p>
  Lorem ipsum dolor sit amet, consectetur adipiscing elit.
  Suspendisse ac ultrices justo. Integer sed ligula euismod,
  consequat ante sit amet, consequat mauris. Quisque vehicula
  est pulvinar tristique rhoncus. Ut mollis tincidunt nisl, non
  mattis diam congue a. Integer sed tortor felis. Etiam vel
  condimentum lacus, vitae adipiscing lacus. Duis consequat diam
  a varius tristique. Pellentesque tempor leo posuere, lacinia
  metus nec, faucibus risus. Aliquam nunc lacus, malesuada et
  elementum sed, feugiat in turpis. Etiam a purus ligula.
  Curabitur vel magna lectus.
</p>

<a name="navthree"></a>
<h3 data-magellan-destination="navthree">Nav Three</h3>

<p>
  Lorem ipsum dolor sit amet, consectetur adipiscing elit.
  Suspendisse ac ultrices justo. Integer sed ligula euismod,
  consequat ante sit amet, consequat mauris. Quisque vehicula
  est pulvinar tristique rhoncus. Ut mollis tincidunt nisl, non
  mattis diam congue a. Integer sed tortor felis. Etiam vel
  condimentum lacus, vitae adipiscing lacus. Duis consequat diam
  a varius tristique. Pellentesque tempor leo posuere, lacinia
  metus nec, faucibus risus. Aliquam nunc lacus, malesuada et
  elementum sed, feugiat in turpis. Etiam a purus ligula.
  Curabitur vel magna lectus.
</p>

<a name="navfour"></a>
<h3 data-magellan-destination="navfour">Nav Four</h3>

<p>
  Lorem ipsum dolor sit amet, consectetur adipiscing elit.
  Suspendisse ac ultrices justo. Integer sed ligula euismod,
  consequat ante sit amet, consequat mauris. Quisque vehicula
  est pulvinar tristique rhoncus. Ut mollis tincidunt nisl, non
  mattis diam congue a. Integer sed tortor felis. Etiam vel
  condimentum lacus, vitae adipiscing lacus. Duis consequat diam
  a varius tristique. Pellentesque tempor leo posuere, lacinia
  metus nec, faucibus risus. Aliquam nunc lacus, malesuada et
  elementum sed, feugiat in turpis. Etiam a purus ligula.
  Curabitur vel magna lectus.
</p>
</div>
</div>
```

Make sure you include the two closing divs at the end and save and reload your browser to see your changes. You will notice that once you scroll the page, the header placeholder image and the nav that it sticks to are at the top of the browser window, and that the nav buttons highlight blue when you scroll to that content on the page. You will also notice that when you click on each of the buttons that you scroll to, both the content and buttons get highlighted. Pretty cool.

Magellan sticky navigation code explanation

There are a lot of things going on here, so let's cover what we just did. We opened a div and gave it an attribute `data-magellan-expedition="fixed"`. This is to make sure the navigation goes sticky or fixed to the top when we scroll past the navigation.

We then have a standard definition list with the class `"sub-nav"`. On each of the list items, we have the attribute `date-magellan-arrival`. This tells the nav button to highlight; when you scroll past this, it highlights the background of the navigation button. Then the link just links to the anchor of the same name, a `<a name="navone">` tag. When you click on the button, it will scroll with an animation to the content. This is done by Foundation and part of the Magellan component.

Off-canvas navigation

We will now cover how to make an off-canvas menu; this type of menu has normally just been used on mobile phones, but over the last year, there have been some sites that have used this type of menu on a tablet and desktop/laptop as well. An off-canvas menu is a menu that slides the content and menu from any side of the screen.

So let's try adding the following code right after the opening body tag:

```
<div class="off-canvas-wrap" data-offcanvas>
    <div class="inner-wrap">
    <nav class="tab-bar">
      <section class="left-small">
      <a class="left-off-canvas-toggle menu-icon" ><span></span></a>
      </section>

      <section class="middle tab-bar-section">
      <h1 class="title">Learning Zurb Foundation</h1>
      </section>
    </nav>
```

```
<aside class="left-off-canvas-menu">
  <ul class="off-canvas-list">
  <li><label>Left Off-canvas</label></li>
  <li><a href="#">Nav One</a></li>
  <li><a href="#">Nav Two</a></li>
  <li><a href="#">Nav Three</a></li>
  <li><a href="#">Nav Four</a></li>
  </ul>
</aside>

<section class="main-section">
```

At the bottom of the file, right before the `<script src="js/vendor/jquery.js">
</script>` code, let's add the following code snippet:

```
    </section>

  <a class="exit-off-canvas"></a>

  </div>
</div>
```

Now, reload your page and you will see another navigation bar above the one we added in an earlier chapter. But you will also see that we have, in the top-left corner, three horizontal lines; this is called a hamburger or hotdog menu. If you click on it, you will see that a menu slides in from the left-hand side. It is not good to have two main navigation bars stacked like this, and we will fix this shortly, but we should cover the code first. We will do this by adding a second off-canvas menu to the right-hand side of the screen.

So let's duplicate lines 20-22 and paste them right below, and then change all the occurrences of left with right, as shown in the following code:

```
<section class="right-small">
    <a class="right-off-canvas-toggle menu-icon" ><span></span></a>
</section>
```

You will see that this now creates a menu in the top-right corner with the same three lines. The next block of code is as follows:

```
<section class="middle tab-bar-section">
    <h1 class="title">Learning Zurb Foundation</h1>
</section>
```

This is where you set the content that shows up in the middle between the menu buttons and takes up the entire width between the menus. Now, we want to actually create the off-canvas menu, so let's copy lines 33-41 and again change left to right, as shown in the following code:

```
<aside class="right-off-canvas-menu">
  <ul class="off-canvas-list">
    <li><label>Right Off-canvas</label></li>
    <li><a href="#">Nav One</a></li>
    <li><a href="#">Nav Two</a></li>
    <li><a href="#">Nav Three</a></li>
    <li><a href="#">Nav Four</a></li>
  </ul>
</aside>
```

Reload your browser and try it out. You will notice that Foundation just handles the off-canvas on the left and right with the code we just typed.

This is pretty cool and all, but having two menus on top of each other is pretty bad, so let's just make the off-canvas menu only show up on a small or mobile screens. To do this, we need to add a couple of classes to some tags to only show the off-canvas on mobiles and also hide the other menu on mobiles.

Thus, on the `tab-bar`, `left-off-canvas-menu`, and `right-off-canvas-menu` div's classes, lets add `"show-for-small"`. You can see this in the following code:

```
      <nav class="tab-bar show-for-small">
<section class="left-small">
  <a class="left-off-canvas-toggle menu-icon" ><span></span></a>
</section>

<section class="right-small">
  <a class="right-off-canvas-toggle menu-icon" ><span></span></a>
</section>

<section class="middle tab-bar-section">
  <h1 class="title">Learning Zurb Foundation</h1>
</section>
</nav>

<aside class="left-off-canvas-menu show-for-small">
  <ul class="off-canvas-list">
    <li><label>Left Off-canvas</label></li>
    <li><a href="#">Nav One</a></li>
```

```
      <li><a href="#">Nav Two</a></li>
      <li><a href="#">Nav Three</a></li>
      <li><a href="#">Nav Four</a></li>
    </ul>
  </aside>

  <aside class="right-off-canvas-menu show-for-small">
    <ul class="off-canvas-list">
      <li><label>Right Off-canvas</label></li>
      <li><a href="#">Nav One</a></li>
      <li><a href="#">Nav Two</a></li>
      <li><a href="#">Nav Three</a></li>
      <li><a href="#">Nav Four</a></li>
    </ul>
  </aside>
```

Then we need to add `"hide-for-small"` in our nav bar. This is on or around line 56 and will look like the following line of code:

```
<nav class="top-bar hide-for-small" data-topbar>
```

Alright, pretty cool! This is how you use off-canvas. Now, let take showing different content on different screen sizes to a whole new level. We will use interchange responsive content. Before we continue, let's remove the show-for-small and hide-for-small tags; you will not need them for the next example.

Interchange responsive content

One of the most useful things about Foundation is the ability to send different content to the device or screen size that the user is viewing your project on. By doing this you can speed up load times, customize the content for a specific device and/or screen size.

So let's give this a shot, right after the div with the class inner-wrap; this will be on or around line 19. Let's add the following code:

```
<div data-interchange="[mobile.html, (small)], [tablet.html,
(medium)], [desktop.html, (large)]"></div>
```

Then we need to create three HTML files called mobile.html, tablet.html, and desktop.html. In index.html. The code you should cut and paste into your mobile.html file is as follows:

```
<nav class="tab-bar">
  <section class="left-small">
```

```
      <a class="left-off-canvas-toggle menu-icon"><span></span></a>
    </section>

    <section class="right-small">
      <a class="right-off-canvas-toggle menu-icon"><span></span></a>
    </section>

    <section class="middle tab-bar-section">
      <h1 class="title">Mobile</h1>
    </section>
  </nav>

  <aside class="left-off-canvas-menu">
    <ul class="off-canvas-list">
      <li>
        <label>Left Off-canvas</label>
      </li>
      <li><a href="#">Nav One</a>
      </li>
      <li><a href="#">Nav Two</a>
      </li>
      <li><a href="#">Nav Three</a>
      </li>
      <li><a href="#">Nav Four</a>
      </li>
    </ul>
  </aside>

  <aside class="right-off-canvas-menu">
    <ul class="off-canvas-list">
      <li>
        <label>right Off-canvas</label>
      </li>
      <li><a href="#">Nav One</a>
      </li>
      <li><a href="#">Nav Two</a>
      </li>
      <li><a href="#">Nav Three</a>
      </li>
      <li><a href="#">Nav Four</a>
      </li>
    </ul>
  </aside>

  <section class="main-section">
```

You will also notice that in the h1 with a class of title, in the middle tab-bar-section tag, the text has been changed to Mobile. This will show the change when we resize our browser window.

Now, let's duplicate this file and call the new file tablet.html, then let's change the h1 heading to tablet, so it should look like the following code:

```
<section class="middle tab-bar-section">
  <h1 class="title">Tablet</h1>
</section>
```

Great, now we need to create a desktop.html file. First let's copy the following line of code from our tablet file:

```
<section class="main-section">
```

Paste it at the top of our desktop.html file and then let's cut the entire nav tag with the class of top-bar and paste it in our desktop.html file. Your desktop.html file should look like the following snippet:

```
<section class="main-section">

        <nav class="top-bar" data-topbar>
      <ul class="title-area">
        <li class="name">
          <h1><a href="#">Logo</a></h1>
        </li>
        <li class="toggle-topbar menu-icon"><a href="#"><span>Nav</
span></a></li>
      </ul>

      <section class="top-bar-section">
        <ul class="left">
          <li class="active"><a href="#">Nav 1</a></li>
          <li class="has-dropdown">
          <a href="#">Nav 2</a>
        <ul class="dropdown">
          <li><a href="#">Nav 2.1</a></li>
          <li><a href="#">Nav 2.2</a></li>
          <li><a href="#">Nav 2.3</a></li>
          <li><a href="#">Nav 2.4</a></li>
        </ul>
          </li>
          <li><a href="#">Nav 3</a></li>
          <li><a href="#">Nav 4</a></li>
          <li><a href="#">Nav 5</a></li>
        </ul>
```

```
        <ul class="right">
          <li><a href="#">Nav 6</a></li>
          <li><a href="#">Nav 7</a></li>
        </ul>

      </section>
    </nav>
```

Now refresh and resize your browser window; you will see that you get the original top bar on the desktop, but when you resize to a tablet or mobile screen, you get the off-canvas menus. This allows you to only send code based on the users screen size and not send it all when you use the show-for and hide-for classes.

Interchange responsive default content

Now, let's say if you do not want to have three files and just want to load something different on mobile, you can delete the tablet.html and desktop.html files from the interchange code in the index file to the following code:

```
<div data-interchange="[mobile.html, (small)]">
  <p>
  Menu Would Go Here
  </p>
</div>
```

You will now see "Menu Would Go Here" when you have your browser window at a desktop and tablet screen size, but when you shrink your site to a mobile phone, it will show the off-canvas menu. Let's undo until we have this code back to the following:

```
<div data-interchange="[mobile.html, (small)], [tablet.html,
(medium)], [desktop.html, (large)]"></div>
```

Interchange responsive images

You can also use interchange on images. This works basically the same way. In the following code, you will see that we have a default image, a large version for, say, the desktop and then we have a retina version. You can also add in small and medium images as well if you need them. You will also notice that right under the image tag there is a noscript tag; you can have a fallback image for browsers that do not support JavaScript:

```
<img data-interchange="[img/default.jpg, (default)], [img/large.jpg,
(large)], [img/retina.jpg, (retina)]">
<noscript><img src="img/fallback.jpg"></noscript>
```

Interchange responsive images with media queries

You will notice in the following code that you can also use custom media queries to send different images based on screen size. If you do not know what media queries are, you can send different content based on different screen sizes, ranges of screen sizes, or whether they are or are not touch devices:

```
<img data-interchange="[/path/to/default.jpg, (only screen and (min-
width: 768px))], [/path/to/bigger-image.jpg, (only screen and (min-
width: 1024px))]">
```

Interchange responsive background images

You can use interchange on background images as well using the following code:

```
<div data-interchange="[img/default.jpg, (default)], [img/small.jpg,
(small)]"></div>
```

Go ahead and try these out for yourself. We will not try these out at this point. The following is a list of all the different options you have to use in the brackets per size:

- In (default) use only screen and (min-width 1px)
- In (small) use only screen and (min-width 1px)
- In (medium) use only screen and (min-width 641px)
- In (large) use only screen and (min-width 1024px)
- In (landscape) use only screen and (orientation: landscape)
- In (portrait) use only screen and (orientation: portrait)

Retina media queries

Retina means a pixel density high enough that the human eye can't see individual pixels at a typical viewing distance. In order to account for this, we need to double the resolution on our images. The following are the media queries to do this for different browser types and resolutions:

- In Webkit use only screen and (-webkit-min-device-pixel-ratio: 2)
- In Firefox use only screen and (min--moz-device-pixel-ratio: 2)
- In Opera use only screen and (-o-min-device-pixel-ratio: 2/1)
- only screen and (min-device-pixel-ratio: 2)
- only screen and (min-resolution: 192dpi)
- only screen and (min-resolution: 2dppx)

Orbit slider

Foundation comes with a slider component that has basically everything you could want with a slider, so let's try it out by creating an unordered list `placehold.it` image on line 23:

```
<div class="row">

    <div class="large-12 columns">
      <ul class="orbit" data-orbit>
        <li>
          <img src="img/wood1.jpg" alt="Wood 1" />
          <div class="orbit-caption">
            This is Wood Panel One
          </div>
        </li>
        <li>
          <img src="img/wood2.jpg" alt="Wood 2" />
          <div class="orbit-caption">
              This is Wood Panel Two
          </div>
        </li>
        <li>
          <img src="img/wood3.jpg" alt="Wood 3" />
          <div class="orbit-caption">
              This is Wood Panel Three
          </div>
        </li>
      </ul>

    </div>

</div>
```

You can use any images you like or you can use the images in the `img` folder at `https://codio.com/kevinhorek/Learning-Zurb-Foundation`.

Go ahead and reload your browser. You will see that your slider works and that it autoplays. You have a caption and three indicator dots that tell you which one of the three slides you are on, under the slider. You can add more than three slides, but we will just use three, since that is the most common one online.

You can also add buttons to change the image. So right below the `ul` code you just added, let's add the following code:

```
<a data-orbit-link="woodone" class="button">
  Wood 1
</a>
<a data-orbit-link="woodtwo" class="button">
  Wood 2
</a>
<a data-orbit-link="woodthree" class="button">
  Wood 3
</a>
```

You will notice that the buttons show up but they do not work. We need to tell the buttons what slide to call. We will do this by adding a `"data-orbit-slide"` attribute to each of the previous `li` tags. So the code will now look like the following snippet:

```
<ul class="orbit" data-orbit>
  <li data-orbit-slide="woodone">
    <img src="img/wood1.jpg" alt="Wood 1" />
    <div class="orbit-caption">
      This is Wood Panel One
    </div>
  </li>
  <li data-orbit-slide="woodtwo">
    <img src="img/wood2.jpg" alt="Wood 2" />
    <div class="orbit-caption">
      This is Wood Panel Two
    </div>
  </li>
  <li data-orbit-slide="woodthree">
    <img src="img/wood3.jpg" alt="Wood 3" />
    <div class="orbit-caption">
      This is Wood Panel Three
    </div>
  /li>
</ul>
```

You will see that each `li` tag has a `"data-orbit-slide"` attribute that matches the button `"data-orbit-link"` attribute on the buttons.

You can also just have text sliders, so let's consider the following code from slide 2:

```
<li data-orbit-slide="woodtwo">
  <img src="img/wood2.jpg" alt="Wood 2" />
  <div class="orbit-caption">
    This is Wood Panel Two
  </div>
</li>
```

We will now change the previous code, as follows:

```
<li data-orbit-slide="woodtwo">
  <h2>I am just text</h2>
  <h3>No Image here</h3>
</li>
```

There are a lot of custom settings you can change on Orbit, and Zurb is always adding new ways to customize Orbit. You should check out the documentation for these settings at `http://foundation.zurb.com/docs/components/orbit.html`.

Clearing

Clearing is a full screen lightbox that is nice to showcase images without the distraction of the other site elements. A good example would be a photograph portfolio gallery. So let's add the following code on or around line 104, just make sure it is above the closing `</section>` tag:

```
<ul class="clearing-thumbs large-block-grid-3" data-clearing>
      <li><a href="img/wood1.jpg"><img data-caption="Wood 1 Caption"
src="img/wood1-tb.jpg"></a></li>
      <li><a href="img/wood2.jpg"><img data-caption="Wood 2 Caption"
src="img/wood2-tb.jpg"></a></li>
      <li><a href="img/wood3.jpg"><img data-caption="Wood 3 Caption"
src="img/wood3-tb.jpg"></a></li>
    </ul>
```

Now, take a look at your browser, you will see three wood paneling images that take up the full width of the browser because we did not put this in the Foundation grid, and when you click on one you get a nice full-screen gallery. You can click through the images, see a caption, and see the thumbnails.

Let's quickly cover the code. This is based on the block grid and you can set how many columns you get for small, medium, and large. Right now we only have three columns showing for the large grid. Then we need to make sure we add the class "clearing-thumbs" and the attribute data-clearing to the ul tag. Then we need to add list items with a link to the full image to show in the gallery. After that, we will add a thumbnail image; this has -tb.jpg and a caption.

If you do not want to show all three images and just have one image clickable to launch the gallery, you can do this by changing the "large-block-grid-3" class to "clearing-feature". Then you need to add the class "clearing-featured-img" to one of the li elements.

Let's duplicate our clearing ul and paste a duplicate and make the changes, as shown in the following code:

```
<ul class="clearing-thumbs clearing-feature" data-clearing>
        <li class="clearing-featured-img"><a href="img/wood1.jpg"><img
data-caption="Wood 1 Caption" src="img/wood1-tb.jpg"></a></li>
        <li><a href="img/wood2.jpg"><img data-caption="Wood 2 Caption"
src="img/wood2-tb.jpg"></a></li>
        <li><a href="img/wood3.jpg"><img data-caption="Wood 3 Caption"
src="img/wood3-tb.jpg"></a></li>
    </ul>
```

You will notice that you have one image now that launches the gallery.

Forms

You might be wondering why we are covering forms in this chapter and not the last chapter. This is because Foundation has a validation library built with JavaScript, so it made more sense to cover them together. So, let's get started with forms on or around line 140; after our clearing code, let's insert the following code:

```
<form>
  <div class="row">
    <div class="large-12 columns">
      <label>Label
        <input type="text" placeholder="I am an input" />
      </label>
    </div>
  </div>
</form>
```

Have a look at that in your browser. Just like all the other elements, you can use the Foundation grid to lay out your forms and put them into different columns to make pretty complicated form layouts. You can put any input, select, or text area element where the input element is currently inside of a label tag. But for radio buttons, you insert your label and then close your label tag and then insert your radio input tags. Let's add the following code on or around line 154:

```
<div class="row">
        <div class="large-6 columns">
            <label>Radio Button Label</label>
            <input type="radio" value="yes" id="yes"><label
for="yes">Yes</label>
            <input type="radio" value="no" id="no"><label
for="no">No</label>
        </div>
</div>
```

If you refresh your browser, you will see our little form coming together. Now, let's add some checkboxes inside that same row. So, on or around line 162, let's add the following code:

```
<div class="large-6 columns">
        <label>Checkbox label</label>
        <input id="checkyes" type="checkbox"><label
for="checkboxyes">Checkbox Yes</label>
        <input id="checkno" type="checkbox"><label
for="checkboxno">Checkbox No</label>
</div>
```

The full row will look like the following code:

```
<div class="row">
  <div class="large-6 columns">
    <label>Radio Button Label</label>
    <input type="radio" value="yes" id="yes">
    <label for="yes">Yes</label>
    <input type="radio" value="no" id="no">
    <label for="no">No</label>
  </div>
  <div class="large-6 columns">
    <label>Checkbox label</label>
    <input id="checkyes" type="checkbox">
    <label for="checkboxyes">Checkbox Yes</label>
    <input id="checkno" type="checkbox">
    <label for="checkboxno">Checkbox No</label>
  </div>
</div>
```

You can also wrap your form in a fieldset, so let's try this out. Let's add a "row" class to our form tag and then add a "fieldset" and a "legend" tag to our form as shown in the following code:

```
<form class="row">
  <fieldset>
  <legend>
    Foundation Forms
  </legend>
  <div class="row">
    <div class="large-12 columns">
      <label>Label
        <input type="text" placeholder="I am an input" />
      </label>
    </div>
  </div>

  <div class="row">
    <div class="large-6 columns">
      <label>Radio Button Label</label>
      <input type="radio" value="yes" id="yes"><label for="yes">Yes</
label>
        <input type="radio" value="no" id="no"><label for="no">No</
label>
    </div>
    <div class="large-6 columns">
      <label>Checkbox label</label>
      <input id="checkyes" type="checkbox"><label
for="checkboxyes">Checkbox Yes</label>
        <input id="checkno" type="checkbox"><label
for="checkboxno">Checkbox No</label>
    </div>
  </div>
  </fieldset>
</form>
```

Make sure you close your "fieldset" tag before the end of the "form" tag. Now, let's make a new row and put our label to the left of our input. In order to do this, let's add the following code on or around line 171:

```
<div class="row">
  <div class="large-2 columns">
    <label for="right-label" class="right inline">Inline label</label>
  </div>
  <div class="large-10 columns">
```

```
        <input type="text" id="right-label">
      </div>
    </div>
```

Foundation also has the ability to create postfixes and prefixes to your input elements. So let's try them out. On or around line 180, let's add the following code:

```
<div class="row collapse">
  <div class="large-2 columns">
    <span class="prefix">Prefix</span>
  </div>
  <div class="large-10 columns">
    <input type="text" placeholder="prefix">
  </div>
</div>
```

Go ahead and refresh. You will see that you have a prefix before your input. Now, let's add a postfix by adding the following code on or around line 189:

```
<div class="row collapse">
  <div class="large-10 columns">
    <input type="text" placeholder="postfix">
  </div>
  <div class="large-2 columns">
    <a href="#" class="button postfix">Postfix Button</a>
  </div>
</div>
```

The postfix is really good for, say, a search field; you will notice that we added a button instead of just a span tag.

Form validation

Now that we have a form, let's add some validation. In order to do this, we need to add a "data-abide" attribute to the form tag. We need to add an error message by adding the following code on or around line 150, right after the label on our first input. It will look like the following code:

```
<div class="row">
  <div class="large-12 columns">
    <label>Label <small>required</small>
      <input type="text" placeholder="I am an input" required />
    </label>
    <small class="error">This is required</small>
  </div>
</div>
```

You will notice that we added the "<small>" tag, which looks like the following line of code:

```
<small class="error">This is required</small>
```

You will also need to add a "required" tag to the input, which will look like the following line of code:

```
<input type="text" placeholder="I am an input" required />
```

Then, on or around line 198, just before the closing "</fieldset>" tag, we need to add a submit button. It will look like the following code:

```
<button type="submit">Submit</button>
```

Now, go to your browser, hit refresh, and click on the **Submit** button. Your form will show an error if you leave that first input empty. Pretty cool right?

Reveal

Reveal is a super useful modal or pop-up window that allows you to display pretty much any type of content from text to images and even video. So let's dive right in and learn how to use Reveal. First we need to create a link that will launch the modal window. So let's do that by adding a link below our form. On or around line 202, after your closing form tag let's add the following code:

```
<p><a href="#" data-reveal-id="modal">Modal</a></p>
```

Now, we need to add the actual modal that loads when you click on the previous link. So right after this line, let's add the following code:

```
<div id="modal" class="reveal-modal" data-reveal>
 <p>I am a modal</p>
  <a class="close-reveal-modal">&#215;</a>
</div>
```

Refresh your browser and you will see a modal link at the bottom and when you click on it you will get your modal. You will notice a cross sign in the top-right corner; if you click on it, you will close the modal. If you want your modal to launch from a button, you can give your link a button class using the following code:

```
<p><a href="#" data-reveal-id="modal" class="button">Modal</a></p>
```

Inside the modal, you can add any HTML you like, even video. You can also control the size of the modal window. You can add any of the following classes after the "reveal-modal" class on the actual modal:

- tiny: Set width to 30 percent
- small: Set width to 40 percent
- medium: Set width to 60 percent
- large: Set width to 70 percent
- xlarge: Set width to 95 percent
- full: Set width to 100 percent

Joyride

Joyride is a powerful way to communicate certain parts of a page to your user. Any element you declare on a page as a Joyride element will get a callout box and you can tour people through the page by these callouts. Let's give them a shot by adding a couple to our site. So, on or around line 212 and after our modal, let's add the following code:

```
<ol class="joyride-list" data-joyride>
  <li data-id="joyride1" data-text="Next" data-options="tip_location:
top">
<h4>Nav 2</h4>
    <p>Here is Nav Two</p>
</li>
  <li data-id="joyride2" data-button="End" data-options="tip_location:
bottom">
    <h4>Nav 3</h4>
    <p>Here is Nav Three</p>
  </li>
</ol>
```

If you refresh your browser, you will notice that nothing happened; that is because we still need to tell Foundation where to add the Joyrides, so let's do that now. So let's find our Nav 2 and Nav 3 elements and add their proper "id's". So on lines 84, we added an ID of "joyride1" and then another of "joyride2" to line 90 with the Nav Three <h3> tag:

```
<h3 data-magellan-destination="navtwo" id="joyride1">Nav Two</h3>
```

You will also need to do one more thing to get Joyride to work; you need to modify the following code:

```
$(document).foundation();
```

This should be found on or around line 319, and you need to call Joyride with JavaScript using the following code:

```
$(document).foundation().foundation('joyride', 'start');
```

Now, go refresh your browser and you will see Joyride working. You will also notice that in the ordered list you can specify where the callout will show up by changing `"data-options="tip_location: top""`. You can set it to `top`, `bottom`, `left`, or `right`.

Accordion

Another common element that you see online is the accordion. This is where you can hide content when you click on a button to show content. So let's get into the accordion by adding the following code after our Joyride code; this will be on or around line 220:

```
<div class="row">

  <dl class="accordion" data-accordion>
    <dd class="accordion-navigation">
      <a href="#accordion1">Accordion 1</a>
      <div id="accordion1" class="content active">
        <div id="accordion1" class="content">
          Accordion 1 content.
        </div>
      </div>
    </dd>
    <dd class="accordion-navigation">
      <a href="#accordion2">Accordion 2</a>
      <div id="accordion2" class="content">
        <div id="accordion2" class="content">
          Accordion 2 content.
        </div>
      </div>
    </dd>
    <dd class="accordion-navigation">
      <a href="#accordion3">Accordion 3</a>
      <div id="accordion3" class="content">
```

```
        <div id="accordion3" class="content">
            Accordion 3 content.
        </div>
        </div>
    </dd>
 </dl>

</div>
```

Now, go ahead and refresh your browser, You will notice that Joyride will scroll you to your first callout, but if you scroll to the bottom of the page you will see your accordion; if you click on the gray bars they will open and close the content. You will also notice that "Accordion 1" is open by default; this is because we set an "active" class on "#accordion1" "id", as shown in the following line of code:

```
<div id="accordion1" class="content active">
```

You can set any or all of the accordions to be active or open, by default, using this class. With accordions, you can add other Foundation elements inside of the hidden content areas. You can also break your accordions up into multiple columns; let's break ours up into two columns. So right after the last accordion, let's create a new one with the following code:

```
<hr />

    <ul class="large-block-grid-2">
        <li>
            <dl class="accordion" data-accordion="2-cols">
                <dd class="accordion-navigation">
                    <a href="#accordion1">Accordion 1</a>
                    <div id="accordion1" class="content">
                        <div id="accordion1" class="content">
                            Accordion 1 content.
                        </div>
                    </div>
                </dd>
                <dd class="accordion-navigation">
                    <a href="#accordion2">Accordion 2</a>
                    <div id="accordion2" class="content">
                        <div id="accordion2" class="content">
                            Accordion 2 content.
                        </div>
                    </div>
                </dd>
            </dl>
```

```
        </li>
        <li>
            <dl class="accordion" data-accordion="2-cols">
                <dd class="accordion-navigation">
                    <a href="#accordion3">Accordion 3</a>
                    <div id="accordion3" class="content active">
                        <div id="accordion1" class="content">
                            Accordion 3 content.
                        </div>
                    </div>
                </dd>
                <dd class="accordion-navigation">
                    <a href="#accordion4">Accordion 4</a>
                    <div id="accordion4" class="content">
                        <div id="accordion2" class="content">
                            Accordion 4 content.
                        </div>
                    </div>
                </dd>
            </dl>
        </li>
    </ul>
```

You will notice that the accordions are now in two columns and work as if they are in one list.

Tabs

Tabs can be a really useful way to handle content, so let's cover how to use tabs. After our accordion code on or around line 294, let's add the following code:

```
<ul class="tabs" data-tab>
  <li class="tab-title active"><a href="#panel1">Tab 1</a></li>
  <li class="tab-title"><a href="#panel2">Tab 2</a></li>
</ul>
  <div class="tabs-content">
    <div class="content active" id="panel1">
      <p>Panel 1</p>
    </div>
    <div class="content" id="panel2">
      <p>Panel 2</p>
    </div>
  </div>
```

Now go ahead and refresh your browser and you will see that you can have two clickable tabs. You can add more tabs by adding or duplicating the `li` tag with `tab-title` and if you add more make sure that you also add the content inside of the `"tabs-content"` div. If you want to make your tabs vertical you can add the `"vertical"` class to after the `"tabs"` and `"tabs-content"` classes. The following is the code example:

```
<ul class="tabs vertical" data-tab>
  <li class="tab-title active"><a href="#panel1">Tab 1</a></li>
  <li class="tab-title"><a href="#panel2">Tab 2</a></li>
</ul>
<div class="tabs-content vertical">
  <div class="content active" id="panel1">
    <p>Panel 1</p>
  </div>
  <div class="content" id="panel2">
    <p>Panel 2</p>
  </div>
</div>
</div>
```

Summary

In this chapter, we covered many JavaScript libraries inside of Foundation, and we talked about how to use them and their different options.

In the next chapter, we will talk about how to test your Foundation projects across modern and outdated browsers, as well as how to test on different screen sizes and devices.

6
Testing

With the Internet today being accessed on devices and computers of all different screen sizes, we really need to test on as many platforms and devices as possible. We are going to cover how to test for the outdated browser and make your project gracefully downgrade or at least make a pop-up message appear telling the user that their outdated browser is not supported by your project anymore. Of course, you are still going to want to test on current modern browsers such as Chrome, Firefox, Safari, and Opera.

We will be covering the following topics in this chapter:

- How to test in all versions of IE
- How to use Microsoft Virtual Machines to test in IE for free
- The devices you should be testing on
- How to test device sizes in Chrome
- Other tools you can try out for testing purposes

Testing IE 6-11

Let's cover what every person that works on the web dreads: testing and making their modern websites work on old versions of IE. We are going to talk about a number of ways to make this process less painful.

Did you know that Microsoft provides you with free virtual machines that have every version of IE installed on them? Well, they do, and you can download them from `http://www.modern.ie/en-us/virtualization-tools`.

Once you go there, you will notice a gray bar area **Download a Virtual Machine. For Mac, Linux, or Windows**. All these are free and when you click on **Get Free VMs**, you will be able to select a platform (Mac, Linux, or Windows). You can see in the next screenshot that **Mac** has been selected. You will also notice that you need to select a virtualization platform and you will be able to select from VirtualBox, VMWare Fusion, and Parallels. All three of these virtualization platforms are great and I have experience with all of them. Let's just use VirtualBox because it is free and cross-platform. If you already own VMWare or Parallels, go ahead and select the one you have currently. If you do not have either, head on over to `https://www.virtualbox.org/wiki/Downloads` and under **VirtualBox platform packages**, select the operating system and download the version for your current system. Then, get it installed.

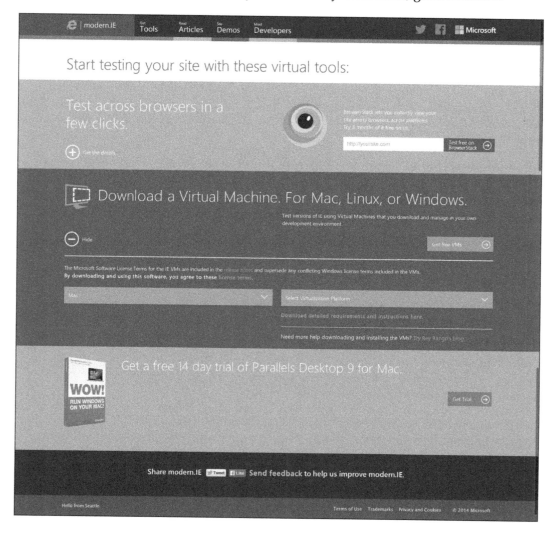

Here comes the part that takes a while. You need to download each part of each IE virtual machine at `http://www.modern.ie/en-us/virtualization-tools`. There are downloading instructions at the bottom of the gray part of the page of the virtual machine software that you selected. Every couple of months, you will need to reactivate your copies of Windows. You will get a pop-up notification and you have to just click on **activate**. This will take a couple of seconds, then it reboots and you are back to your testing.

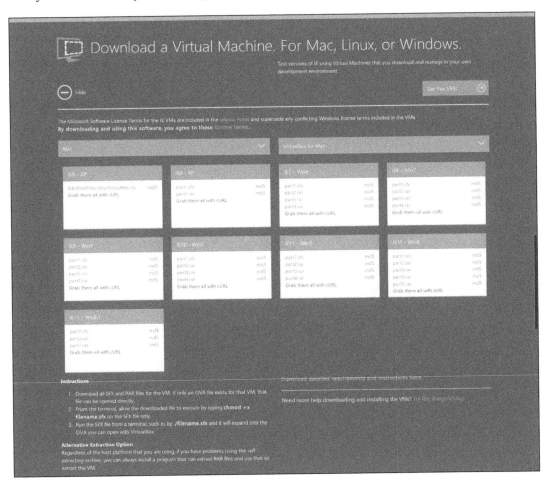

Once you follow the installation instructions and get them all installed, you should see the following screenshot in your VirtualBox:

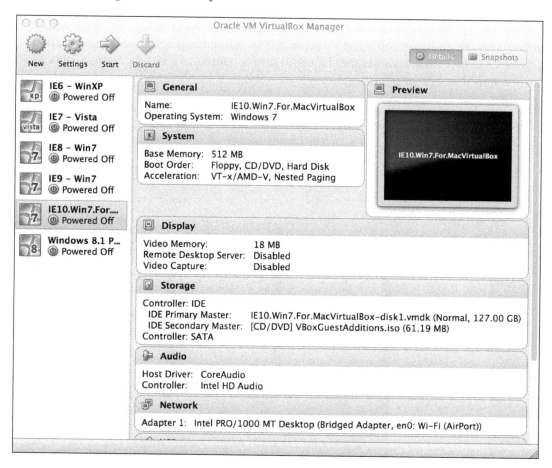

Once you have them all listed, select **Settings** on each one and then hit the
Network tab and you should change **Attached to** to **Bridged Adapter**, as shown
in the following screenshot:

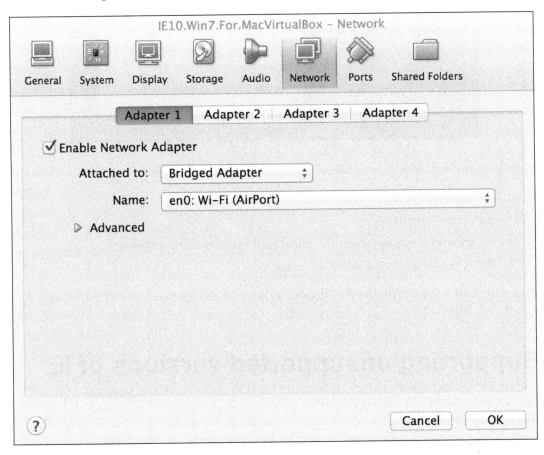

This will allow you to be able to call your project by your computer's local IP and
get Internet access to your virtual machine to test sites that are live on the Internet.
Now all you need to do is double-click on one of the virtual machines and it will
launch Windows with the IE version that comes with that version of Windows.

The next thing you need to do is install guest additions, as shown in the following screenshot:

Installing guest additions will allow you to accomplish the following:

- You no longer have to capture the mouse pointer
- Set your resolution
- Copy and paste between the guest and host operating systems
- Run Windows in the seamless mode

You will need to perform guest additions to each of the virtual machines that you install in VirtualBox.

Supporting unsupported versions of IE

Foundation 4 and 5 both dropped support for IE8, and for a lot of projects, you can get away with not supporting IE version 6, 7, and 8. However, what happens if you need some of the functionality in Foundation 5 and also need to support IE8. Well, here are some ideas to do this. Bryan Thrasher came up with this really great solution to get the grid working in IE8 http://foundation.zurb.com/forum/posts/2049-simple-solution-for-ie8-and-foundation-5.

It involves some additional HTML, CSS, and jQuery but it can be a lifesaver. There is also a grid fix for IE8 for Foundation 4 that can be downloaded from https://gist.github.com/hatefulcrawdad/5068210. Basically, it forces IE8 to support the grid and does a pretty good job.

Testing IE7 and IE6

If you need to support IE7, you can either go to `http://foundation.zurb.com/docs/` and scroll to the bottom, and download and use an older version of Foundation, Version 2 supports IE7, or you can set the Foundation 2 grid classes and Foundation 5 classes in their HTML file, then perform some simple browser detection either on the server or with JavaScript/jQuery, and then send the user either the Foundation 5 files or if the user is using an older version of IE, the Foundation 2 files. This might not be ideal but I have seen it being done, and for certain types of projects, this might enable you to use the latest version and let your outdated browser users still have a good experience.

Foundation has never supported IE6, and it is so unlikely that you will need to support IE6 that there is not really anything you can do with Foundation to make it work with IE6. If you need to support IE6, I would suggest either not using Foundation or building a special table-based site with as few features as possible and send that to your IE6 users with some browser detection.

For any older version of IE that you are not supporting, you should give the user a message that says the site they are currently on does not support their browser and that they should upgrade. A really handy little site that will give you some JavaScript to help you out with this is `http://www.browser-update.org/`.

You can select the versions of older browsers you want a message to show up on and you just cut and paste the a script into your website.

Multiple device testing

You can simulate responsive design by resizing your browser window and see how your project resizes based on the browser window size. However, you should still test on the actual devices that your user base will be using. You can easily find out this information by looking at the site's current analytics and seeing what their users are coming to their site with. You can also use a tool available at `http://caniuse.com/usage_table.php` to see which browser versions are popular. If they come to the site with a device you do not have, you might want to think strongly about getting that device. Personally, I have found that even device simulators are not always accurate about what happens on the actual device. So, the following is a list of devices that your project should be tested on:

- iPhone 4/4s – this is more for load times and site speed
- iPhone 5
- An Android device running Android 2.3

- An Android device running Android 4.0 or higher
- iPad
- Nexus 7

You should either be able to use some of your old devices, borrow a device or two from a friend, or pick up some used devices on eBay. There are a few places that rent out devices by the hour or day, and you can go there and test on pretty much anything you can dream of. A lot of these places get their devices donated and allow developers the opportunity to test on these devices. You can also use online tools at `http://www.responsinator.com/`, but I still find that you need to test on the actual device to make sure what you are building works properly.

Another thing that you could do is go to an electronics store and pull up your project on the test devices and see whether there are any issues with your project.

Remote debugging

Did you know that you can connect both your Android and iOS devices to the computer and use the web inspector on your computer to help you debug your layout issues? The following are some really good posts:

- Android posts can be found at `https://developers.google.com/chrome-developer-tools/docs/remote-debugging`
- iOS posts can be found at `https://github.com/google/ios-webkit-debug-proxy`
- Adobe also has their own app for this called Adobe Edge Inspect, which you can read about at `http://html.adobe.com/edge/inspect/`

If you are willing to spend a little more money, you can get something called Ghostlab (`http://vanamco.com/ghostlab/`). Anytime you do anything on your computer, your browsers and devices will automatically update it. I have used this and it works pretty well. You should at least download the trial version and see if it can be added to your workflow.

Chrome simulation

A new feature that was added to the Chrome development tools is the ability to emulate a bunch of devices. We just talked about how emulation cannot always provide you with accurate results when viewing the same page on the actual device, but it is worth noting because it can be good to at least see something on a simulator instead of nothing at all.

So, make sure that you have the Chrome developer tools open. If you do not know how to open **Developer Tools**, go to the top-right corner of your browser, click on the three horizontal lines ▦, then go to **Tools**, and then select **Developer Tools**.

In the top-right corner of the developer tools, you will see a gear, as shown in the following screenshot:

Select the gear and make sure that under **Appearance, Show 'Emulation' view in console drawer** is checked, as shown in the following screenshot:

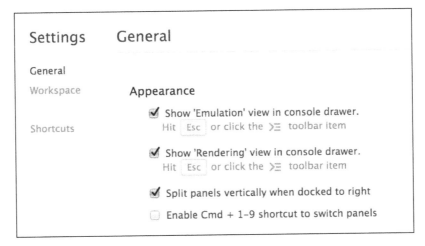

Click on the icon that looks like an arrow and three horizontal lines, to the left of the gear, as shown in the following screenshot:

Click on it and it will bring up another panel. Then, click on **Emulation**. You will notice that there is a select box with a listing of a bunch of devices. You can select a device and then click on **Emulate**, the page you are currently viewing will now be emulated like it was on that particular device. Pretty cool!

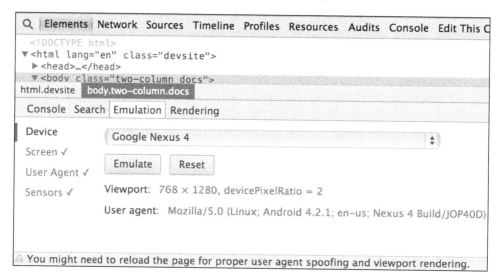

Now that we have covered how to test on multiple devices, go ahead and try out some of these new ways to test your projects.

Other tools you can try out for testing purposes

The following is a list of other tools you can use for testing purposes:

- The Responsive Inspector extension for Chrome available at `http://outof.me/responsive-inspector-beta-released/`
- Online Android Emulator available at `http://www.genymotion.com/`
- Sauce Labs, a Web and mobile app testing available at `https://saucelabs.com/`
- Keynote, a mobile testing app available at `http://www.keynote.com/solutions/testing/mobile-testing`
- BrowserStack, a web-based browser testing available at `http://www.browserstack.com/`

Summary

We covered some cost-effective ways to test your projects across devices and browsers. We also talked about the best way to test multiple versions of IE and how to do this on one computer. Then, we covered which devices to test on and how to emulate devices that you do not have so that you can at least see how things will look on these devices. In the next chapter, we will cover how to use Sass with Foundation.

7
Sass and Foundation

If you are looking to speed up your code and extend your CSS, you can use Sass, and since Foundation uses Sass, we will be covering how to use Foundation and Sass in this chapter.

If you want to read more about the Sass project, you can visit the project's website at http://sass-lang.com. This site will keep you up to date on new features of Sass and has documented how to use every possible feature. As this is not a book about Sass, we will learn how to install Sass with Foundation and get it up and running in a free online code editor so that setting it up will be a lot easier if you are new to Sass.

We will also cover the very basics of Sass, but if you want to get more familiar with Sass outside of this book, there are some really good tools and ways to install Sass on your machine at http://sass-lang.com/install. On the left-hand side of the page, there are free and paid cross-platform apps to get you compiling Sass quickly without knowing any command line, and on the right, you will see how to get Sass working with the command line.

If you want to learn how Foundation uses Sass, as long as you follow along, you will be fine and learn about it as we work through this chapter. Then, you can visit the previous given link and try out other features of Sass on your own.

We will cover the following topics in this chapter:

- What exactly is Sass?
- Installing Foundation with Sass
- Going over the default settings file
- Going over the files

Introducing Sass

If you understand CSS even at a basic level, you will understand Sass, or SCSS as it used to or still can be called. SCSS was a way to write Sass without the brackets, but they have deprecated this, so we will not be using it.

When you write Sass, you are basically writing CSS in a slightly different way. Sass files are compiled to a CSS file, and this compiled CSS file is what you include in your project, just like you have since you started using an external CSS file. Do not let Sass scare you. Even if you never use all the advanced features and just learn how to nest and use variables; these are two of the most powerful, basic, and simple Sass concepts to wrap your head around.

So, what exactly is Sass? Basically, it takes everything that CSS has to offer and gives you a bunch of extra things to extend the functionality and saves you a lot of time when writing CSS. For example, you can nest CSS classes so that you do not have to write the same classes over and over again to keep targeting elements inside that element. Let's go through a quick example of nesting. Do not worry about coding anything yet; let's just go through some basics first.

Currently, this is how you would target the h1 and p tags inside the .header class:

```
.header h1 {
  font-size: 34px
}

.header p {
  font-size: 14px
}
```

There is nothing wrong with doing it this way, but with Sass and nesting, we can write less code to get the same results, and when Sass compiles this code, it will output the same CSS as it did previously. The following code is what the Sass version of the same .header class would look like:

```
.header {
  h1 {
    font-size: 34px;
  }

  p {
    font-size: 14px;
  }
}
```

Pretty cool and simple, right? You will notice the indentation of the code; this is not a Sass-specific thing. We do this so that it looks cleaner and is easier to read.

You can also style, say, the background color of the `.header` class inside the same nesting tag as follows:

```
.header {
  background: blue;

  h1 {
    font-size: 34px;
  }

  p {
    font-size: 14px;
  }
}
```

You will notice that in the previous code, there is `background: blue;` but there is no closing bracket on the next line. This is not needed because this closing bracket is actually at the bottom of the tag and it is the second one after the p tag. You can also nest multiple classes and tags inside each other. The following is an example:

```
.header {
  background: blue;

  h1 {
    font-size: 34px;

    span {
      color: red;
    }
  }

  p {
    font-size: 14px;
  }
}
```

You will see that inside the h1 tag, we nested a span tag. This changes the color of the text inside the header class h1 span tags to red.

There are a bunch of things you can do with nesting, but let's cover another simple concept. Let's say you want all your `h1` tags throughout your project to be red and use the font size of 34 px. You also want any `h1` tags with the class of `.subheader` to be blue and use the font size of 18 px. Let's review how you would write this. In your HTML file, you should have `<h1>` as follows:

```
<h1>Heading one</h1>
```

We will also have `h1` with the class of `.subheader` as shown in the following code:

```
<h1 class="subheader">Sub Header</h1>
```

Your Sass code will be as follows:

```
h1 {
  color: red;
  font-size: 43px;

  &.subheader {
    color: blue;
    font-size: 18px;
  }
}
```

You will notice that the `.subheader` class has `&` before it. This tells Sass that the subheader class is in the `h1` tag. If the subheader class was, say, on the span tag inside `h1`, we will not use `&` and either change `&` to a span tag or just delete it.

All nesting works with IDs in the same way as it does with classes, and as you can already see, using only nesting is a concept that is not really different from how you currently write your CSS, but this saves you a lot of time when coding your projects.

Installing Foundation with Sass

To get the Sass version of Foundation, you need visit `http://foundation.zurb.com/docs/sass.html`. You will notice that you need to have the following tools already installed on your system:

- Git (`http://git-scm.com/`)
- Ruby 1.9+ (`https://www.ruby-lang.org/`)
- NodeJS (`http://nodejs.org/`)
- You must also be comfortable with the command line

If they are already installed on your system go ahead use your own setup for this chapter. If you have never heard of these tools or do not feel comfortable with any of them, do not worry. You do not need them for this book or to learn how to use the Sass version of Foundation because we will use the free version of the online editor available at https://codio.com/. They have most of this stuff installed for you by default and this will get us up and running quickly without getting too technical.

So, let's get going with our installation of the Foundation version of Sass. If you are following along with the book, make sure that you have created an account at https://codio.com/ and are logged in at https://codio.com/ followed by your username you signed up with. Mine is https://codio.com/kevinhorek and you can follow along with the book at this URL.

If you are following along exactly with the book, you should be logged in and your dashboard page should look something like the following screenshot:

Select **Create Project** and under **Project Name**, type in `Learning Zurb Foundation`. Make sure that the **Public** radio button is selected and that you have **empty project** selected under **Choose a template** in the **Template** section, as shown in the following screenshot:

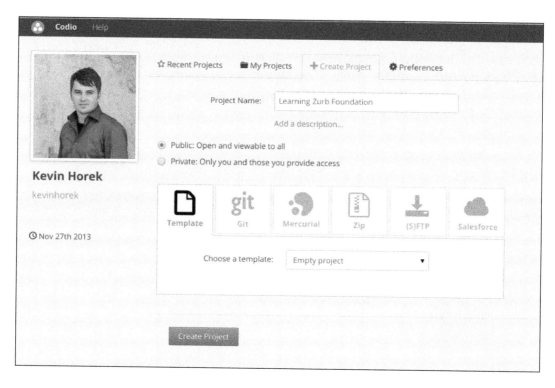

Then, click on the **Create Project** button. This will take you into the code editor, which will look like what's shown in the following screenshot; mine has the previous chapters in folders on the right-hand side.

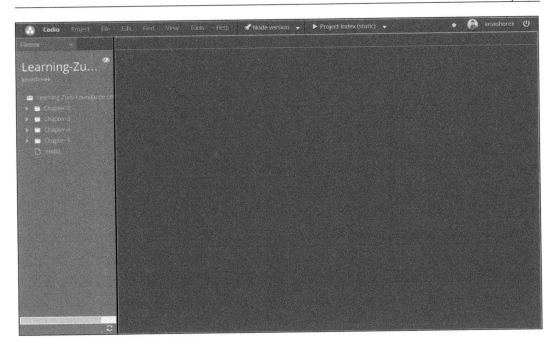

Perfect! Now, this is where we start installing the Sass version of Foundation in Codio or using another editor on your local computer.

For those of you that are following along with the book in Codio, select **Tools** and then click on **Terminal** in the top menu. If you are using your computer, open your command line and type the following command:

```
npm install -g bower grunt-cli
```

If you are not using Codio you might need to type sudo in front of npm.

Bower is a package manager and Grunt is a task manager. So, Zurb puts Foundation into Bower so that it is easier to update and uses Grunt so that it can compile your Sass. This will take a minute or so to finish. When it does, type the following command:

```
gem install foundation
```

This should take a few seconds. Then, if you are not using Codio, change your directory into the directory that you want to put this Foundation with Sass project. If you are on a Mac machine, the command will be as follows:

```
cd Sites/GIVEYOURPROJECTANAME
```

If you are on Windows, the command will be as follows:

```
cd C:\users\{your name}\Documents
```

Once you are in the directory you want this chapter in, or in Codio just the terminal, type in:

```
foundation new Chapter-7 --libsass
```

This will take a minute or so, and if you are using Codio or your own editor, change into your project folder by using the following command:

```
cd Chapter-7
```

Then, type in the following code:

```
grunt build
```

You should see the following output:

```
Running "sass:dist" (sass) task
File "css/app.css" created.
Done, without errors.
```

Before we test Foundation with Sass, let's cover a couple things that we just installed:

- We just installed Grunt, a JavaScript task manager; you can view the project at http://gruntjs.com/
- Libsass, a Sass compiler, which you can view at https://github.com/hcatlin/libsass

We will not be covering either of these tools in this book, but you should check out each of the links so that you can understand what is happening and what each of these tools do. Especially Grunt, as it is very popular right now and can do a lot of things for you, similar to some of the software that is listed at http://sass-lang.com/install in the left column. You just need to figure out which workflow works best for you and your team.

In Codio or your editor, open the project folder and click on the index.html file in your editor. Then, if you are in Codio, it might say **Project Index (static)** on the top bar; click on the arrow to the right, and it will drop down into a menu. Select the current file inside Codio, as shown in the following screenshot:

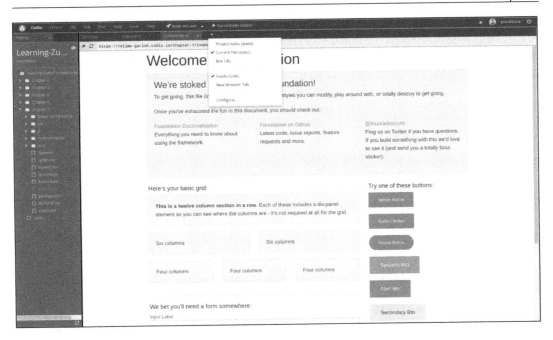

You should see the default Foundation site, as seen in the previous screenshot. If you are not using Codio, you can just double-click on the index.html file in the project folder and it will open in your default browser.

Going over the default settings file

Now, let's make sure that Sass is working and try making a change to the Foundation Sass variables file. So, in the Sass folder, open the _settings.scss file. This is the extension of a Sass file. There are two ways you can write Sass, and therefore, you might see Sass files with the extension of .sass. This allows you to write Sass without any semicolons and curly brackets, and spacing of your code becomes more important. We will not cover this in this book because Foundation is not using this format and it is deprecated and not that common anymore, but it should be mentioned.

Now that you have the _settings.scss file open, you will notice two things. First, there is an underscore in the file name; this is to show that this file is being included. It is not needed. It is just a nice visual way to show which files are getting included. The second thing you will see is a long file with most of it commented out. These are default variables that you can change in the Sass version of Foundation.

Variables are simply information that you want to store and use over and over again. For example, it is hard to remember certain hex color values. So, instead of looking them up every time you need it, or copying them from somewhere else, create that color as a variable and you can call that variable in your Sass. When the Sass file gets compiled, it will put in the right hex value for you. We will be using variables throughout this book. The following is an example of a color variable:

```
$primary-color: #8d0024;
```

You would put this at the top of any of your Sass files. So, to use this color in your project, you will use the variable in your Sass file as follows:

```
background: $primary-color;
```

Let's start off by changing the background of the body tag to red. This is on line 42 of the file, and once you delete the two slashes, the line should look this:

```
// We use these to control various global styles
$body-bg: red;
// $body-font-color: #222;
// $body-font-family: "Helvetica Neue", "Helvetica", Helvetica, Arial,
sans-serif;
// $body-font-weight: normal;
// $body-font-style: normal;
```

Now in Codio, go to your current file's tab or reload your index.html file in your browser. If you are not using Codio, you will see that the site's background is red. If you go to the Codio terminal tab or your terminal/command line, you will see that something changed in your _settings.scss file and that it was compiled without errors, as shown in the following screenshot:

```
codio@relime-garish:~/workspace$ cd Chapter-7
codio@relime-garish:~/workspace/Chapter-7$ grunt
Running "sass:dist" (sass) task
File "css/app.css" created.

Running "watch" task
Waiting...OK
>> File "scss/_settings.scss" changed.

Running "sass:dist" (sass) task
File "css/app.css" created.

Done, without errors.
Completed in 1.271s at Sun Apr 13 2014 19:55:35 GMT+0000 (UTC) - Waiting...
```

If you had an error where Done, without errors is, it will be either yellow for a warning or red for an error. Errors usually mean that there is something wrong in your Sass like a typo, a missed semicolon, or a missing curly bracket. Having Sass show your errors while you are coding your SCSS is super helpful and you should get used to seeing them. Sass will usually give you a line number and sometimes even hint at what is wrong, if it can't compile your files.

We can go ahead and set that variable back to #fff or just comment it out and tell Sass that you just want to use the default, which is #fff.

Covering the variables

Now, let's start from the top of this Sass variables file and cover what is in this file. The variables start on line 9, with a comment explaining that the default body font size in Foundation 5 is going to be using rem's as a font size but Foundation wants to use a default pixel font size to base all your rem values off. So, basically 1rem will be the same as 16 px. However, if you uncomment the $rem-base value and set the value to 18 px, then 1rem will be 18 px. Basically, Foundation is using a formula to make sure that whatever you set your $rem-base variable pixel value to, it will be equal to 1rem.

Then, from line 15-24, you will see a few comments and two variables that you can change to make the base font size not be 100 percent of the rem-base variable. Play with this number and see what results you get. The next thing you will see is that you can also change how the line height is calculated; this is on line 24. You can leave most of the these values as they are, but you might want to change them. If you do not change them, they will just stay as default values.

Lines 26-29 allow you to change where you want to include the html, print, and global classes in your project. It is likely that you will never modify these, but if you do not want to use the Foundation print CSS classes, you might want to uncomment it and set true to false. This is where things really start to get interesting. You can modify the grid of Foundation and set the maximum width of your site by setting the $row-width value on line 36 to a value higher than 1,000. Then, you can also control how many columns there are in your site on line 37. You should not need more than 12 columns, but if you do, for instance, working on a newspaper layout, you might want to have more columns.

If you remember from *Chapter 2, The Foundation Grid*, we talked about there being three grid sizes: small, medium, and large. However, there are two more: xlarge and xxlarge. These can be turned on using line 34, and you can start using them in your project. We will cover this a little more in the next chapter.

Now that we have covered the grid, let's talk about some of the global variables that you can change inside this file.

Between lines 41-49, you can change the general body options, such as body background color, like we tried a while back. Then, you can change font options such as color, family, weight, style, and smoothing, as shown in the following code:

```
// We use these to control various global styles
// $body-bg: #fff;
// $body-font-color: #222;
// $body-font-family: "Helvetica Neue", "Helvetica", Helvetica, Arial,
sans-serif;
// $body-font-weight: normal;
// $body-font-style: normal;
// We use this to control font-smoothing
// $font-smoothing: antialiased;
```

Next, between lines 51-54, you have the ability to change the text direction so that your text will read from right to left instead of left to right. This is extremely helpful if you are in certain parts of the world or are doing a project for those parts of the world that read from right to left. You can also change the default float of elements to accommodate the right to left text direction, as shown in the following code:

```
// We use these to control text direction settings
// $text-direction: ltr;
// $opposite-direction: right;
// $default-float: left;
```

It is between lines 56-62 where things really start to get interesting. You can set a few default colors that will change and automatically theme parts of Foundation just by changing the hex values on lines 57-62. These are just Sass variables Foundation has used and allows you to, say, change $primary-color to green and $secondary-color to black and hit save. Lines 56-63 should look as follows:

```
// We use these as default colors throughout
// $primary-color: #048661; //
// $secondary-color: #e7e7e7;
// $alert-color: #f04124;
// $success-color: #43AC6A;
// $warning-color: #f08a24;
// $info-color: #a0d3e8;
```

Then, in Codio, go to the current file tab of your browser and hit refresh and you will see that your default Foundation theme now takes the specified shade of green as the primary color and turns a bunch of the elements to green or a shade of that green. You will also see that your secondary button is black. We will cover how to add your own variables later in the next chapter, but for now, let's keep going through the file:

```
// We use these as default colors throughout
$primary-color: green;
$secondary-color: black;
// $alert-color: #f04124;
// $success-color: #43AC6A;
// $warning-color: #f08a24;
// $info-color: #a0d3e8;
```

Lines 64-66 allow you to change the radius and rounded corners of any element you give the class of radius or rounded to. If you uncomment either of these values and change them, save the file, and go to your current file tab or refresh in your browser, you will see that the radius button and/or the rounded button on the right-hand side column have been modified to accommodate your changes, as shown in the following code:

```
// We use these to make sure border radius matches unless we want it
different.
// $global-radius: 3px;
// $global-rounded: 1000px;
```

Between lines 68-71, you can change the inset edge on certain elements. Go ahead and play around with these if you like:

```
// We use these to control inset shadow shiny edges and depressions.
// $shiny-edge-size: 0 1px 0;
// $shiny-edge-color: rgba(#fff, .5);
// $shiny-edge-active-color: rgba(#000, .2);
```

Now, on line 73, the gutter variable allows you to change the spacing between the grid columns. You will likely change this to a bigger or smaller value on some of your projects:

```
// $column-gutter: rem-calc(30);
```

Between lines 75-105, you have a bunch of media query options and you can control the range of all the different grid sizes, as shown in the following code. This is super powerful and useful on certain project types. Then, you can see that Foundation has a bunch of built-in media queries and ways to target landscape, portrait, or grid range. We will cover these in more detail in the next chapter:

```
// Media Query Ranges
// $small-range: (0em, 40em);
// $medium-range: (40.063em, 64em);
// $large-range: (64.063em, 90em);
// $xlarge-range: (90.063em, 120em);
// $xxlarge-range: (120.063em, 99999999em);

// $screen: "only screen";

// $landscape: "#{$screen} and (orientation: landscape)";
// $portrait: "#{$screen} and (orientation: portrait)";

// $small-up: $screen;
// $small-only: "#{$screen} and (max-width: #{upper-bound($small-
range)})";

// $medium-up: "#{$screen} and (min-width:#{lower-bound($medium-
range)})";
// $medium-only: "#{$screen} and (min-width:#{lower-bound($medium-
range)}) and (max-width:#{upper-bound($medium-range)})";

// $large-up: "#{$screen} and (min-width:#{lower-bound($large-
range)})";
// $large-only: "#{$screen} and (min-width:#{lower-bound($large-
range)}) and (max-width:#{upper-bound($large-range)})";

// $xlarge-up: "#{$screen} and (min-width:#{lower-bound($xlarge-
range)})";
// $xlarge-only: "#{$screen} and (min-width:#{lower-bound($xlarge-
range)}) and (max-width:#{upper-bound($xlarge-range)})";

// $xxlarge-up: "#{$screen} and (min-width:#{lower-bound($xxlarge-
range)})";
// $xxlarge-only: "#{$screen} and (min-width:#{lower-bound($xxlarge-
range)}) and (max-width:#{upper-bound($xxlarge-range)})";

// Legacy
// $small: $medium-up;
// $medium: $medium-up;
// $large: $large-up;
```

Between lines 107-112, you can customize your default cursors (you usually never change them unless you have a specific reason to do so), as shown in the following code:

```
//We use this as cursors values for enabling the option of having
custom cursors in the whole site's stylesheet
// $cursor-crosshair-value: crosshair;
// $cursor-default-value: default;
// $cursor-pointer-value: pointer;
// $cursor-help-value: help;
// $cursor-text-value: text;
```

Next up is typography. There are a lot of variables you can change from lines 115-218. They are all self-explanatory, but we should cover a few of the cooler things that are happening in some of these variables. Have a look at line 140. The `$subheader-font-color: scale-color($header-font-color, $lightness: 35%)` element is technically a mixin and we will cover this in the next chapter; you will see a scale color; this is how you can use different shades of a color based on another variable. You will see that line 140 uses the color variable of `$header-font-color`. At line 124, you will see that the color is set to `#222`, and then, it sets that color to be 35 percent lighter with the `$lightness: 35%` attribute. If you use a positive number, the color will be lighter, and if you use a negative number, the color will be darker:

```
// TYPOGRAPHY
//

// $include-html-type-classes: $include-html-classes;

// We use these to control header font styles
// $header-font-family: $body-font-family;
// $header-font-weight: normal;
// $header-font-style: normal;
// $header-font-color: #222;
// $header-line-height: 1.4;
// $header-top-margin: .2rem;
// $header-bottom-margin: .5rem;
// $header-text-rendering: optimizeLegibility;

// We use these to control header font sizes
// $h1-font-size: rem-calc(44);
// $h2-font-size: rem-calc(37);
// $h3-font-size: rem-calc(27);
// $h4-font-size: rem-calc(23);
// $h5-font-size: rem-calc(18);
// $h6-font-size: 1rem;
```

```
// These control how subheaders are styled.
// $subheader-line-height: 1.4;
// $subheader-font-color: scale-color($header-font-color, $lightness:
35%);
// $subheader-font-weight: normal;
// $subheader-top-margin: .2rem;
// $subheader-bottom-margin: .5rem;

// A general <small> styling
// $small-font-size: 60%;
// $small-font-color: scale-color($header-font-color, $lightness:
35%);

// We use these to style paragraphs
// $paragraph-font-family: inherit;
// $paragraph-font-weight: normal;
// $paragraph-font-size: 1rem;
// $paragraph-line-height: 1.6;
// $paragraph-margin-bottom: rem-calc(20);
// $paragraph-aside-font-size: rem-calc(14);
// $paragraph-aside-line-height: 1.35;
// $paragraph-aside-font-style: italic;
// $paragraph-text-rendering: optimizeLegibility;

// We use these to style <code> tags
// $code-color: scale-color($alert-color, $lightness: -27%);
// $code-font-family: Consolas, 'Liberation Mono', Courier, monospace;
// $code-font-weight: bold;

// We use these to style anchors
// $anchor-text-decoration: none;
// $anchor-font-color: $primary-color;
// $anchor-font-color-hover: scale-color($primary-color, $lightness:
-14%);

// We use these to style the <hr> element
// $hr-border-width: 1px;
// $hr-border-style: solid;
// $hr-border-color: #ddd;
// $hr-margin: rem-calc(20);

// We use these to style lists
// $list-style-position: outside;
```

```
// $list-side-margin: 1.1rem;
// $list-ordered-side-margin: 1.4rem;
// $list-side-margin-no-bullet: 0;
// $list-nested-margin: rem-calc(20);
// $definition-list-header-weight: bold;
// $definition-list-header-margin-bottom: .3rem;
// $definition-list-margin-bottom: rem-calc(12);


// We use these to style blockquotes
// $blockquote-font-color: scale-color($header-font-color, $lightness:
35%);
// $blockquote-padding: rem-calc(9 20 0 19);
// $blockquote-border: 1px solid #ddd;
// $blockquote-cite-font-size: rem-calc(13);
// $blockquote-cite-font-color: scale-color($header-font-color,
$lightness: 23%);
// $blockquote-cite-link-color: $blockquote-cite-font-color;


// Acronym styles
// $acronym-underline: 1px dotted #ddd;


// We use these to control padding and margin
// $microformat-padding: rem-calc(10 12);
// $microformat-margin: rem-calc(0 0 20 0);


// We use these to control the border styles
// $microformat-border-width: 1px;
// $microformat-border-style: solid;
// $microformat-border-color: #ddd;


// We use these to control full name font styles
// $microformat-fullname-font-weight: bold;
// $microformat-fullname-font-size: rem-calc(15);


// We use this to control the summary font styles
// $microformat-summary-font-weight: bold;


// We use this to control abbr padding
// $microformat-abbr-padding: rem-calc(0 1);


// We use this to control abbr font styles
// $microformat-abbr-font-weight: bold;
// $microformat-abbr-font-decoration: none;
```

The other thing you will notice is that you can do some basic math on variables. These are best outlined between lines 973-999. You will see that a variable has another variable inside it and then the variable present inside is being multiplied by a number, or the size of that variable is getting changed by the `rem-cal` value of a number.

This `_settings.scss` file is almost 1,300 lines. So, we will not cover them all because a lot of them are clearly commented and you will not remember them all. The thing to remember is that Foundation with Sass has tons of variables, and instead of creating a custom Sass file to override a default in Foundation, you should check this file first and make sure that there is not one already set up and built in for you to change. You will need to be careful if you update to a new version of Foundation. You will likely have to merge your old file with the new file; this is so you do not override your changes to your current file. Chances are that you will not update Foundation if you are doing project-based work, but if you are using it at a startup, you will be updating Foundation all the time, and would also think you would be using some kind of version control to make sure that you have versions of everything, so that if you do override something you can get it back.

Going over the files

You will also notice that there is an `app.scss` file in the `scss` folder. Let's open this up and cover what is in this file. Once this file is open, you will see on line 1 that this is where the `_settings.scss` file is being included. You will also notice that when referring to the settings file, you do not need to include `_` or `.scss`. Between lines 4-40 you have a bunch of commented-out Foundation components. This allows you to only use and include the parts of Foundation you need per project. So how you use this is you comment out line 2 and then uncomment line 5, and then uncomment the lines you need in your project. Just make sure that you have a comma after each line and that you have a semicolon after the last uncommented line. By only including the components you are using in a project, you can cut your CSS files down in file size quite a bit. Only use this when you feel more comfortable with Foundation. So for this book, we will always include all of Foundation code like on line 2 of this file.

The index file

Now, let's open the `index.html` file in the root of our project directory. The only real differences you will notice in the `index.html` file, as we are using the Sass version of Foundation compared to the default version we were using in the previous chapters, are the JavaScript files that are now being put in the `bower_components` folder and called from that folder. If you are not familiar with Bower, it is a package manager for the Web and you can read more about it at `http://bower.io/`. If you do not know what a package manager is, it is not really going to affect your progress with this book, but you should read up on what Bower is and how it can save your time when building your web projects on Bower. If you open the `bower_components` folder, you will see a bunch of JS libraries, Foundation, JQuery, and a few other JS libraries that Foundation needs to run. The libraries are being managed and installed through the Bower Package Manager. We installed Bower when we were installing the Sass version of Foundation.

If you leave that folder and go back to your root project directory, you will see a CSS folder. If you open that folder, you will see an `app.css` file; this is different from the file we used before. In the previous chapters, we included a `foundation.css` file. Zurb changed the name of this due to the fact that when you are using Sass, you can include other CSS or Sass libraries in your application, so it is likely that you are not just using Foundation. If this does not make sense, it will later when we cover how to add your own files to your Sass project. So let's get back to the `app.css` file. Open it up and you will notice that the file is on one line or just a jumbled mess without any comments or spacing. This is called minifying your code. What minifying does is strip out all the spacing, formatting, and comments, that is, basically all the stuff that the browser does not need to interrupt the file. Some of the benefits of minifying your files are to increase page speed and reduce the CSS download time.

So, the cool thing about how Foundation with Sass is set up is that you use the `app.scss` file in the `scss` folder, make your code readable by using spacing and comments, and then when your `app.css` file gets generated every time, you hit save. It combines all the files in your SCSS folder, minifies all the files, and then puts them all together into the `css/app.css` file. If you are new to this, it can be confusing to wrap your head around. If you do not quite get this yet, that is fine. Once we code further, we will cover this concept in more detail, and you will start to get it.

How do my files get converted?

You are likely wondering how these .scss files are getting converted to the app. css file, and it is a great question and there are multiple ways to convert your .scss files to .css files. There are a bunch of applications that will handle it for you and they are listed and updated on the official Sass install page at http://sass-lang. com/install. In Foundation with Sass, Zurb uses something called Grunt to compile your Sass automatically when you hit save. You, of course, have to tell Grunt to check your Sass folder for changes on save, but we will cover that in a while. Let's cover what Grunt is first. Grunt is a JavaScript Task Runner and the project can be viewed at http://gruntjs.com/. What is a JavaScript Task Runner? Simply put, it automates repetitive tasks for you. So, in our case, Grunt watches our SCSS folder and whenever we make a change to one of the files in that folder and hit save, Grunt puts all the files in the SCSS folder into one file, minifies the code, and then overrides the app.css file in our css folder. This app.css file is the file that we include in our index.html page and the browser styles our page with this file.

What is Grunt?

At the time of writing this book, there are over 2,000 tasks or plugins that Grunt can do for you and are listed at http://gruntjs.com/plugins. Let's open the Gruntfile.js file in the root of our project directory just so you understand better what is happening. This is also where you can add other tasks or plugins you get from the previous link.

So, in Gruntfile.js, on line 7, it is calling to Foundation that was installed through Bower earlier. This is the core of Foundation and you should never modify the files in any of the folders under bower_components. Then, you will see that it compresses elements present on line 5, and on line 26, it includes the SCSS app.scss file, the one we are making theming changes in, and then outputs it into css/app.css. The following is the code:

```
sass: {
    options: {
      includePaths: ['bower_components/foundation/scss']
    },
    dist: {
      options: {
        outputStyle: 'compressed'
      },
      files: {
        'css/app.css': 'scss/app.scss'
```

```
        }
      }
    },

    watch: {
      grunt: { files: ['Gruntfile.js'] },

      sass: {
        files: 'scss/**/*.scss',
        tasks: ['sass']
      }
    }
  }
```

Why is the setup so complicated?

By now, you must be thinking, "Boy, why is this so complicated?" Well, it is complicated, but once you use all this stuff a few times and understand it, the time you save on your projects will be well worth the time it took to fully understand it. This is the main reason why we set up this chapter's code in Codio and not on your local machine. If you are new to this stuff, it might be overwhelming but keep using Codio for your Foundation with Sass projects. Then, once you fully understand it, try installing all the parts listed at the beginning of this chapter on your local machine and get it running. You will really understand what Codio is doing for you when you start to move outside of it and onto your local machine. There are simpler ways to use Sass, but Foundation is not using them. So, we are going through how to use Foundation with Sass in the simplest way we can by using an online editor (Codio) and you can view my code through this as well. Codio has a free version, and you can read more about it at https://codio.com/s/pricing/.

Let's review the JS files

You will also notice a js folder with an app.js file; this is where you can put all your custom JavaScript for the project. If you open this file, you will notice that it is just calling Foundation.

You will also notice that there is a node_modules folder and it has a bunch of additional folders. These are just Node modules that are needed for Sass and Grunt; you should not worry about having to touch anything in there.

You will also notice a few other files in the root of the project directory, which are as follows:

- `.bowerrc`: This tells the project the directory to the Bower components.

- `.gitignore`: If you are using Git, this is where you tell Git not to commit the files and folders that are listed in this file.

- `bower.json`: This will specify dependencies. You will never change this file.

- `Gruntfile.js`: This has been covered previously.

- `humans.txt`: You can write project notes or anything else that is relevant to the project to let other people working on the project know about it.

- `index.html`: This has been covered previously.

- `package.json`: This is where you can specify a specific version of any of the modules in `node_modules`.

- `README.md`: This has install instructions, we covered these at the beginning of the chapter; the only thing we did not cover was cloning Foundation from Git. It is a little outside of this book and to be honest, you can do what we did and then push it to a Git repository, so you can still use Git with this project.

- `robots.txt`: This is where you can control which parts of your projects web crawlers can go and index your site. There are a lot of really good tutorials online if you just search for robots.txt tutorials on Google.

Summary

There you have it. This is the basics of Sass with Foundation. We covered how to get Sass installed and how to get it up and running. We also went through all the files and started changing some Sass variables. In the next chapter, we will move our one-page website into our Sass version and start customizing it and make the site look pretty. Also in the next chapter, we will cover mixins; these can take Sass to the next level.

8
Mixins

Now that we have Sass up and running and you are familiar with it, let's take it to the next level, where you can really start to see the power and reusability of Sass. When creating mixins, you will need to think about reusability and there are lots of mixin libraries out there that you can use for your projects.

We will be covering the following topics in this chapter:

- What are mixins?
- Using mixins within Sass and Foundation
- Mixin libraries and other useful mixins

What are mixins?

Mixins are blocks of code that you can reuse multiple times and when Sass gets compiled, they will be included and written out. Let's have a look at a simple mixin:

```
@mixin transition {
  -webkit-transition: all 0.3s ease;
  -moz-transition: all 0.3s ease;
  -ms-transition: all 0.3s ease;
  -o-transition: all 0.3s ease;
  transition: all 0.3s ease;
}
```

Now, let's talk about the previous code. First, you will see `@mixin`. You need this on every mixin you create, as this tells Sass you are declaring a mixin. Then, you will see `transition`. This is just a name to describe what the mixin is for; it can be anything you like. As this mixin is for the transition CSS attribute, we will call it `transition`. If it was for rounded corners, we would call it something like `@mixin rounded-corners {}`. Now, you will see plain old CSS for all the different browser prefixes. Prefixes are used to make sure that all of the browsers can recognize the `transition` attribute. Now that we have the `transition` mixin, we can use this mixin over and over again on all our projects. We can either cut and paste the mixin into every project we need transitions in, or we can create a master mixins file, put all our mixins in that, and just delete the ones we will not be using on that project. You would then import this file into your project.

Ok, great! We have a transition mixin, but what if you want to change the transition to transition only a certain property or change the duration or what type of transition? Well, you can. Let's modify the previous mixin to allow for this, and then we will cover how to actually use this in your project:

```
@mixin transition($element: all, $time: 0.3s, $animation: ease) {
    -webkit-transition: $element $time $animation;
    -moz-transition: $element $time $animation;
    -ms-transition: $element $time $animation;
    -o-transition: $element $time $animation;
    transition: $element $time $animation;
}
```

Now, let's discuss the previous code. You will see that we added a bracket after `transition` and some variables such as `element`, `time`, and `animation` which are just names. They can be anything, but try and make them descriptive about what they are for. This makes your code more readable for others and also yourself if you need to make changes to your project months later. You will then see a colon and a default value. You can change the default when you call the mixin; we will cover this shortly. You will then notice that in each of the CSS cross-browser attributes, we put each of the variable names to pull the value that we put in there, and if we do not insert a value, it will put the default value. Also, if you want to just change one or two of the attributes, you can do that. So, let's say you just want to change the time; it would look like this:

```
@mixin transition($time: 0.3s) {
    -webkit-transition: all $time ease;
    -moz-transition: all $time ease;
    -ms-transition: all $time ease;
    -o-transition: all $time ease;
    transition: all $time ease;
}
```

Pretty cool! Now, let's cover how you include these in your code. Let's add this transition to a button class:

```
.button {
        @include transition($element: all, $time: 0.5s, $animation:
        ease-in);
}
```

You could also write the previous code as follows:

```
.button {
        @includetransition(all,0.5,ease-in);
}
```

You will see that we change the time and the animation on the button transition. Now, there is another way you can write this mixin, as shown in the following code:

```
@mixin transition($attributes) {
  -webkit-transition: $attributes;
  -moz-transition: $attributes;
  -ms-transition: $attributes;
  -o-transition: $attributes;
  transition: $attributes;
}
```

You will see that we just defined one variable and that we can fill in the three attributes when we call this mixin like this:

```
.button {
        @include transition(all .5s ease-in);
}
```

Personally, I like this way best. It is easier for me to wrap my head around this, and when defining variables, you need to write the attributes in the proper order. If you put a number variable where you should be putting the transition type, the mixin will throw an error. So, for easier debugging, just specifying what is required when calling the mixin works better for me. However, this is really your call. Try using both and see what you prefer.

Before we start playing with some mixins, let's cover another example to understand the basics, how powerful and useful mixins can be, and how they can save you a lot of time. With mixins, you can also create and include multiple CSS blocks of code, as shown in the following code:

```
@mixin password-strength {
  .password-strength {
    position: absolute;
```

```
    top: 60px;
    padding: 5px 0;

    @media handheld, only screen and (max-width: 767px) {
      top: 80px;
    }
  }

  @media handheld, only screen and (max-width: 767px) {
    label.password {
      padding-top: 20px;
    }
  }

  .password-strength-bad {
    color: $color-red;
  }

  .password-strength-ok {
    color: $color-yellow;
  }

  .password-strength-good {
    color: $color-green;
  }
}
```

You can see from the preceding code that we are creating a `password-strength` mixin with multiple states and a position based on some media queries on devices or handhelds. Then, let's say you want to include this inside `form` with a panel inside, you would use the following code:

```
form {
      .panel {
            @include password-strength();
      }
}
```

Any panel inside a `form` tag will automatically get all the password strength mixin code when Sass gets compiled into CSS. This way, you can reuse that same password strength anywhere else in your code, and you only have to update it in one place. You will also notice that you can use variables inside your mixins as used in `password strength` previously.

Now that we have covered the basics of mixins, let's start using them with Foundation and start doing some things together.

Using a mixin within Sass and Foundation

Foundation has many ways to use mixins within Sass. You can just write your own, as we did previously, and include them in your SCSS, or you can take many of the Foundation components and build your own custom components. When you combine your own Sass, mixins, media queries, and Foundation components, you can pretty much do anything you like layout- and theme-wise. This is what makes Foundation the most advanced responsive framework.

When you think of mobile first and start to get into Sass and mixins, you will start to put the bare minimum on the screen on mobile, and then, as the screen size gets bigger, you might decide to add more polish to certain elements. For example, you might round the corners, add a gradient, and give the text a shadow on a button when it is on a desktop. You have the ability to only add custom SCSS on different screen sizes. This level of customization can allow you to control every aspect of your project for any resolution.

Let's try some stuff together. To get things going fast, either duplicate your `chapter 7` folder and rename it to `chapter 8`, or if you are using Codio, open your terminal by going to **Tool** and then select the terminal. Make sure you are at `:~/workspace$` and then type in `foundation new Chapter-8 --libsass`. Codio should now have created a new project with Foundation, Sass, and Grunt in the `chapter 8` folder.

Now, let's open our `index.html` file in this folder and either preview it in the browser or select the current tab in the top menu bar if you are using Codio. If you need to follow along, you can see my code at `https://codio.com/kevinhorek/ Learning-Zurb-Foundation`. It will be under the **Chapter 8** folder.

Now that we have a fresh version of Foundation, let's try out some mixins on this default theme. First, let's open the `app.scss` file in the `scss` folder, and after line 2, add the following line:

```
@import "theme";
```

So, the final code should look like the following:

```
@import "settings";
@import "foundation";
@import "theme";
```

You need to make sure you import the settings first, then Foundation, and then your theme. If you mix the order up, you will get unexpected results.

Below this, you will see a bunch of commented-out foundation components. Then, in the scss folder, let's create a new file and call it _theme.scss. If you remember from the last chapter, _ is not needed but it just tells you that this is an imported file. Now that the file is created, open it up, and if you are using Codio, you should see something like the following code in the file:

```
/*
    Document    : Chapter-8/scss/theme.scss
    Created on : 2014-04-25 01:47 AM
    Author      : kevinhorek
    Description:
    Purpose of the stylesheet follows.
    To change this template use Tools | Templates.
*/


root {
    display: block;
}
```

Let's delete all of this. It is nice that Codio automatically adds this comment so that you can leave some information about the file. However, just to keep things consistent for those of you who are not using Codio, delete everything so that we are all starting out with a blank file. If you do not want to delete everything, make a backup of this file and then delete your code.

Let's go back to our terminal and type in cd Chapter 8, then type in grunt. This will make Grunt compile your Sass file to CSS, so we can see our changes. The following is a screenshot of what you should see:

```
codio@relime-garish:~/workspace$ cd Chapter-8
codio@relime-garish:~/workspace/Chapter-8$ grunt
Running "sass:dist" (sass) task
File "css/app.css" created.

Running "watch" task
Waiting...
```

Now, let's use Sass and some mixins to build our own custom Foundation component. On line 19, you will see the following code:

```
<div class="panel">
```

Let's change the panel class to custom-block:

```
<div class="custom-block">
```

Then, refresh your browser. You will see that the gray border and background are gone. So, let's start building our own custom panel that we can reuse in anything later on.

Make sure that you are in your _theme.scss file. Let's add the following code:

```
.custom-block {
  $panel-bg: scale-color(#43ac6a, $lightness: -5%);
  $panel-border-style: double;
  $panel-border-size: 4px;

  @include panel($padding: 50px);
}
```

Then, refresh your browser and you will see that you have a green panel with a darker green double border. Then, you will see that the value of padding of this element is 50px. The following is the CSS that gets generated:

```
.custom-block {
        border-style: double;
        border-width: 4px;
        border-color: #399158;
        margin-bottom: 1.25rem;
        padding: 50px;
        background: #40a364;
}
```

Let's take a second to break down this code. In the .custom-block class, you will see the following three lines:

```
$panel-bg: scale-color(#43ac6a, $lightness: -5%);
$panel-border-style: double;
$panel-border-size: 4px;
```

If you want to read more about Foundation's mixins, you can visit http://foundation.zurb.com/docs/components/global.html. These are Sass Foundation variables that Zurb has set up for customization for you; they have these for every component.

Then, you will see the following code:

```
@include panel($padding: 50px);
```

This is where you include the actual Foundation panel mixin which actually only gives you three attributes that you can customize when you include the panel mixin. These are shown in the following code:

```
$bg, $padding:20px, and $adjust:true
```

The first two mixin variables are self-explanatory, but the third one does not really makes sense. It is an option to set the font color to automatically change based on the darkness of the background color. So you should always keep this set to `true`, so never include it because it is `true` by default.

Hopefully by now, you are starting to see that by combining the Foundation Sass variables and the Foundation mixins, you can create some very custom components. When creating these custom components, you need to make sure that you declare all your variables first and then you include your mixin. If you do not do this, the code will not work.

So, as you can see from the previous example, we declare all our variables first, as shown in the following code:

```
.custom-block {
  $panel-bg: scale-color(#43ac6a, $lightness: -5%);
  $panel-border-style: double;
  $panel-border-size: 4px;

  @include panel($padding: 50px);
}
```

Then, we include the mixin, which in this case, is called `panel`. We include this because we want to pull the variables from the code we just specified previously in the `.custom-block`.

Now, let's customize this panel a lot more. Let's round the corners of this panel by using a custom mixin. In our `_theme.scss` file, create a mixin to handle the rounded corners cross-browser, and then include this mixin in our panel.

So, at the top of our `_theme.scss` file, starting from line one, add the following code:

```
@mixin rounded ($radius: .8em) {
  -webkit-border-radius: $radius;
  -moz-border-radius: $radius;
  border-radius: $radius;
}
```

Now that we added this in, let's include these rounded corners in our panel, so add the following code:

```
@include rounded();
```

Add the previous code below the `panel` mixin:

```
.custom-block {
    $panel-bg: scale-color(#43ac6a, $lightness: -5%);
    $panel-border-style: double;
    $panel-border-size: 4px;

    @include panel($padding: 50px);

    @include rounded();
}
```

You will notice that in `@include rounded();`, we are not specifying a radius, so it will pull the `.8em` for the mixin that we created on line 1, which is as follows:

```
@mixin rounded ($radius: .8em) {
    -webkit-border-radius: $radius;
    -moz-border-radius: $radius;
    border-radius: $radius;
}
```

Let's change the radius to `2em`, so the code will look as the following code:

```
@mixin rounded ($radius: .8em) {
    -webkit-border-radius: $radius;
    -moz-border-radius: $radius;
    border-radius: $radius;
}
.custom-block {
    $panel-bg: scale-color(#43ac6a, $lightness: -5%);
    $panel-border-style: double;
    $panel-border-size: 4px;

    @include panel($padding: 50px);

    @include rounded($radius: 2em);
}
```

You will notice that we are overriding the default value of `.8em` with `2em` when we include the rounded mixin. This should be on or around line 14.

Hopefully, by now you are starting to get how to use Sass with mixins and variables to make some pretty custom theming options. You should try to do your own custom mixins within Sass.

Instead of covering every component and how to customize them with mixins, you should really just check out the components documentation on the Foundation website at `http://foundation.zurb.com/docs`. If you select a component from the left-hand side and scroll down close to the bottom of this page, you will see the Sass variables you can customize and how to use the mixin to implement that component. We could talk about each of them, but Zurb is very active with their development of Foundation and keep their documentation up to date and are always adding new things to Foundation. Since this book started, there have been a lot of changes, and additional components have been added. So, if you want to keep up on all the changes that have been happening to Foundation, you should really be checking their monthly changelog at `http://foundation.zurb.com/docs/changelog.html`.

Mixin libraries and other useful mixins

As you can see, Foundation has many ways to use and build your own mixins but there are a lot of mixins and mixin libraries out there that you might find useful for your projects. So, let's cover some of them:

- Sass mixins available at `http://sass-lang.com/documentation/file.SASS_REFERENCE.html#mixins`
- Bourbon is a Sass mixin library, available at `http://bourbon.io/`
- Sassy buttons available at `http://jaredhardy.com/sassy-buttons/`
- Sass CSS3 mixins available at `http://mynameismatthieu.com/sass-css3-mixins/`
- *8 Sass mixins you must have in your toolbox* is available at `http://zerosixthree.se/8-sass-mixins-you-must-have-in-your-toolbox/`

Summary

As you can see, there are a lot of ways to use and customize Foundation and Sass with mixins. Try using mixins on your next Sass project; they will save you a lot of time, and as you get more familiar with them, you will find even more creative ways to mix and mash them together to do some remarkable things.

In this chapter, we covered what mixins are, how to use them with Sass and Foundation, and we talked about some mixin libraries and some other useful mixins. In the next chapter, we will give you some ideas on how to create responsive design.

Designing Responsive Ideas

_9_

We have dedicated pretty much the entire book to how to use Foundation and the different components that the framework comes with, but now, we should talk about how to design pages with Foundation. If you are not a designer, you will still find this chapter useful, and what you learn in this chapter should help you make nicer looking projects or, at the very least, understand where a designer is coming from when they are designing.

We will be covering the following topics in this chapter:

- Using Foundation for in-browser designs
- Building a quick prototype
- Reviewing the prototype
- Customizing the prototype
- Foundation theme
- Creating Foundation grids in Photoshop

Using Foundation for in-browser designs

For practice, let's set up a new project again for Foundation. For those of you who are following along with the book in Codio, select **Tools** and then **Command bar** from the top menu.

If you are using your computer, open your command prompt and type the following command:

```
npm install -g bower grunt-cli
```

If you are not using Codio, you might need to type the following command:

```
sudo in front of npm.
```

This will take a minute or so to finish; when it does, type the following:

```
gem install foundation
```

This should take a few seconds. If you are not using Codio, go to the directory where you want to put this Foundation with the Sass project. The command will be something like the following if you are on a Mac machine:

```
cd Sites/GIVEYOURPROJECTANAME
```

The command will be something like the following if you are on Windows:

```
cd C:\users\{your name}\Documents
```

Once you are in the directory, you want this chapter in or in Codio just the terminal, type in Chapter-9:

```
foundation new Chapter-9 --libsass
```

This will take a minute or so. Then, if you are using Codio or your own editor, go to your project folder using the following command:

```
cd project-name
```

Now, type in the following:

```
grunt build
```

Now that we have everything set up, let's go to the SASS folder, open the app.scss file, and add the following right after @import "foundation";:

```
@import "theme";
```

This is a great way to extend and theme Foundation without changing the core or the actual Foundation files. This also makes it a lot easier to update your version of Foundation. Zurb pushes new features and bug fixes on a pretty regular basis.

Now, your file should look like this:

```
@import "settings";
@import "foundation";
@import "theme";
```

You will also notice that you have a bunch of commented components of Foundation that start on line 5 with the following:

```
// Or selectively include components
```

Each component of Foundation can be included on a per-project basis. You include only what you are using in the project so that you do not load extra components into the project that you are not using. Only including what you are using will speed up page loading, especially on mobile. Also, you can only include the JavaScripts that you need; this is out of the scope of this book, but I do encourage you to get comfortable with Foundation first and then try to include only what you need.

Once you feel comfortable with Foundation, you would comment out the following:

```
@import "settings";
@import "foundation";
@import "theme";
```

Then you would include certain components. Just make sure you uncomment line 6. Then you would uncomment the following lines because you just want grid and type:

```
@import
"foundation/components/grid",
"foundation/components/type";
```

You will notice that after the grid, there is a comma (,), and when you are at the last import, you have a semicolon (;). For the sake of this book, I deleted all the other imports that are commented out; you can leave them commented or deleted. I prefer to leave them commented as Sass removes the comments when it compiles the CSS files. This makes it easier for you to import additional components later if the project requires it.

If you want to just include the JavaScript that you are using, delete the following from the bottom of your index.html file:

```
<script src="/js/foundation.min.js"></script>
```

Now, add the following code there:

```
<script src="/js/foundation.js"></script>
```

After this line, you can add each of the components you want, as shown in the following code:

```
<script src="/js/foundation.js"></script>
<script src="/js/foundation.dropdown.js"></script>
etc...
```

To find out where all the .js files are, you need to look in the js folder and then inside the foundation folder. Once you are inside the foundation folder, you will see foundation.js and foundation.dropdown.js.

Building a quick prototype

Now that we have imported the `theme.scss` file, we need to actually create that file. So, let's create a `_theme.scss` file in the `scss` folder. Open this file, and if you are using Codio, you should see the following:

```
/*

    Document    : Chapter-9/scss/_theme.scss
    Created on  : 2014-05-12 04:22 AM
    Author      : kevinhorek
    Description:
    Purpose of the stylesheet follows.
    To change this template use Tools | Templates.
*/


root {
    display: block;
}
```

Let's delete everything in this file. It is good to have these comments, but to make sure that you can follow along with Codio or your own editor, we are deleting them.

Now, let's switch back to the terminal and type `grunt`. This will make sure that our Sass is getting compiled and that we will see our changes. Now that we have Sass running, let's talk about how to design in a browser.

Let's open the `index.html` file, delete lines 17 to 157, and add the following code on or around line 17:

```
<div class="row">

    <nav class="top-bar" data-topbar>
      <ul class="title-area">
      <li class="name">
      </li>
      <li class="toggle-topbar menu-icon"><a href="#"><span>Menu</
span></a></li>
      </ul>

      <section class="top-bar-section">
      <ul class="left">
        <li><a href="#">Button 1</a></li>
        <li><a href="#">Button 2</a></li>
        <li><a href="#">Button 3</a></li>
        <li><a href="#">Button 4</a></li>
```

```
    </ul>
    </section>
  </nav>

</div>
```

Refresh your browser, and you will see that we have a header area and a navigation bar. This is shown in the following screenshot:

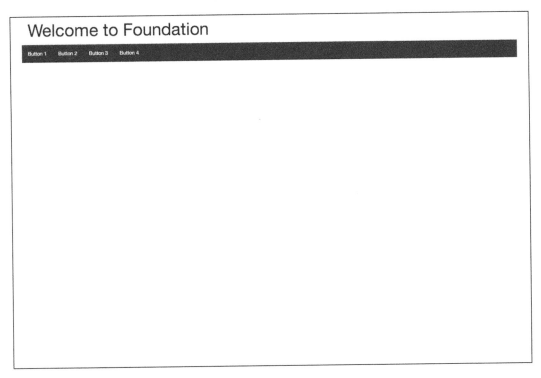

Next, let's create a main header, subheader, and some introduction text, and add a photo on the right-hand side of the page.

On line 38, let's add the following; you do not have to add all the lorem ipsum in the paragraph tag:

```
<div class="row">

    <div class="small-12 medium-6 large-6 columns">
        <h1>Main Heading</h1>
        <h3 class="subheader">Sub Heading</h3>
```

```
            <p>Lorem ipsum dolor sit amet, consectetur adipiscing
elit. Sed dapibus accumsan mauris sodales lacinia. Aliquam id tellus
eget lorem pellentesque viverra at ut nisi. Donec fermentum eros est,
in dictum purus condimentum in.</p>
        </div>
```

Now, before we refresh our browser, let's add the photo right below the last div:

```
<div class="small-12 medium-6 large-6 columns">
    <div class="panel photo">
        Photo
    </div>
</div>

    </div>
```

Now, let's go to the browser and refresh the page. You should see our site looking like what is shown in the following screenshot:

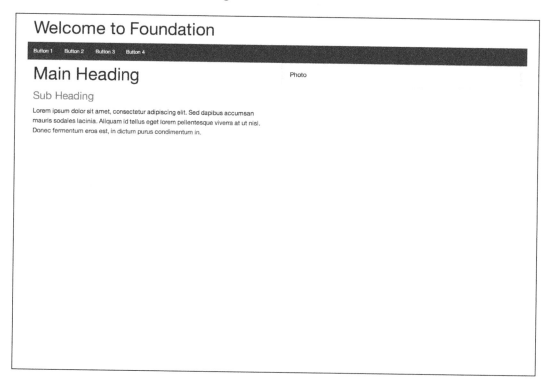

Great! Now that we have the previous code working, let's add three featured calls to actions. On line 53, let's add the following. Remember that you can create the first featured item and copy and paste the code for the other two:

```
<div class="row featured">
    <hr />
        <div class="small-12 medium-6 large-4 columns">
            <div class="panel">
                <div class="row">
                    <div class="large-6 columns">
                        <img src="http://placehold.it/190x190">
                    </div>
                    <div class="large-6 columns">
                        <h4>Featured Title</h4>
                        <p>The featured item description would go
here. It would continue here.</p>
                        <p><a href="#" class="button">View Item</a></p>
                    </div>
                </div>
            </div>
        </div>
        <div class="small-12 medium-6 large-4 columns">
            <div class="panel">
                <div class="row">
                    <div class="large-6 columns">
                        <img src="http://placehold.it/190x190">
                    </div>
                    <div class="large-6 columns">
                        <h4>Featured Title</h4>
                        <p>The featured item description would go
here. It would continue here.</p>
                        <p><a href="#" class="button">View Item</a></p>
                    </div>
                </div>
            </div>
        </div>
        <div class="small-12 medium-6 large-4 columns">
            <div class="panel">
                <div class="row">
                    <div class="large-6 columns">
                        <img src="http://placehold.it/190x190">
                    </div>
```

```
                <div class="large-6 columns">
                    <h4>Featured Title</h4>
                    <p>The featured item description would go
here. It would continue here.</p>
                    <p><a href="#" class="button">View Item</a></p>
                </div>
            </div>
        </div>
    </div>
</div>
```

Now, go to your browser and refresh the page, and you will see what's shown in the following screenshot:

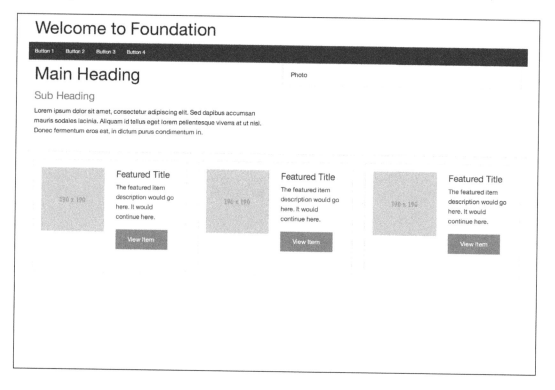

You might be wondering what `http://placehold.it/190x190` is. Basically, this will generate gray placeholder boxes to simulate an image placeholder. I like to use this to quickly show where images will go, especially when I am making responsive prototypes. You would not let your projects go live with these in them.

Great! We have a working site, but let's add a footer. On line 99, let's add:

```
<div class="footer">
    <div class="row">
        <div class="small-12 medium-12 large-12 columns">
            <p class="right">&copy; 2014</p>
        </div>
    </div>
</div>
```

Now, refresh your browser, and you can see that we have a basic site layout pretty quickly:

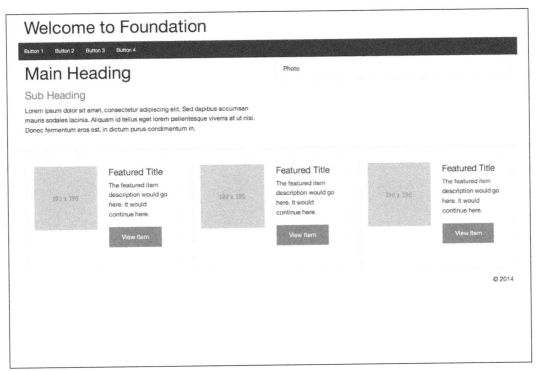

Reviewing the prototype

Now that was fast! We have a quick layout of a home page with a navigation bar, some introduction text, a photo, three featured callouts, and a simple footer. As you can see, this looks like stock Foundation, but you can see how fast it can be to get something that works on large, medium, and small screen sizes.

Here is a screenshot of what this will look like on a phone:

As you can see, our design is pretty responsive right now. There will be a few things that you will want to do, such as add some padding, change the colors, and maybe add some other design elements. However, you have a working responsive prototype right now. At this point, you can start getting your team's feedback on your design; they can give you feedback, you can incorporate their changes and add some polish such as some padding, and then, you can show your client the responsive prototype. When you present a responsive prototype, you need to make it clear that what you are showing them is a basic layout of their project and that colors, fonts, images, and so on are yet to be added.

What you are presenting is how the project will work and look on different screen sizes. I recommend that you create three to five pages and make sure you link them to each other in the navigation, so when you are presenting these to a client and/or your team, you can show them your prototype on a desktop/laptop, tablet, and phone. This will truly help the client understand exactly what they will be getting. This also allows the client to give you any feedback on elements, copy, and images that should appear on each of these screens. You then can add these into the prototype and get their sign off.

Once you have the clients sign off on this prototype, you can then take this prototype and start adding colors, fonts, images, copy, and so on.

Customizing the prototype

Now that we have a working responsive prototype, let's give this one page a little styling love.

Let's open the `settings.scss` file in the `scss` folder. On line 57, let's remove `//` and change it to the following:

```
$primary-color: #048661;
```

Once you refresh your browser, you will see that buttons go green, as shown in the following screenshot:

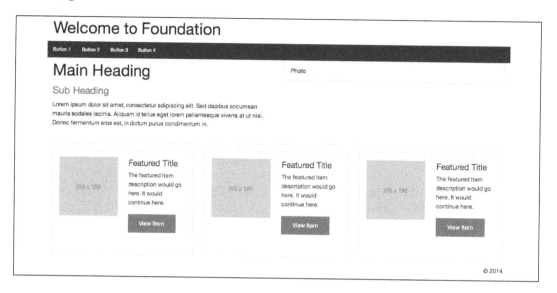

Now, let's remove // and change line 36 to the following:

```
$row-width: rem-calc(1280);
```

Make sure that your browser window is wider than the width of the site, and you will see that our site gets wider. Like we covered in *Chapter 7, Sass and Foundation*, you can see how changing a couple of values in the Foundation settings file can make some pretty big changes to your project.

Now, let's remove the gray background on the panels. On line 805, let's change it to:

```
$panel-bg: #fff;
```

You will see that the panel's gray background is gone. Now, let's open the _theme. scss file and add the following:

```
.top-bar {
  background: $primary-color;

  .top-bar-section {
    display: table;
    margin: auto;

    ul {
      display: table-cell;
```

```
li {

    &:not(.has-form) a:not(.button) {
      background: $primary-color;
      font-size: 1.2rem;
    }

    &:not(.has-form) a:not(.button):hover {
      background: #000;
    }
  }

  }
 }


}
```

You will see that the navigation now is centered, green, and has a hover state that goes black when you hover over one of the buttons. See the following screenshot first; then, we will review the code:

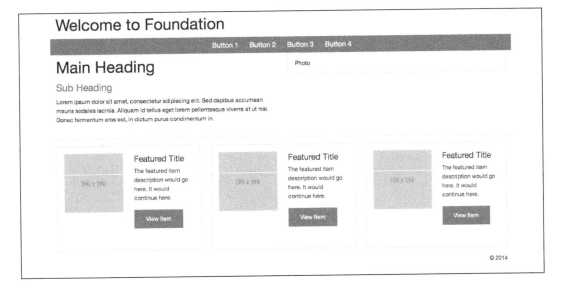

You might be wondering where we are getting the crazy targeting from. All you need to do is right-click on any element in Chrome and select **Inspect Element**. You will now see the page as shown in the following screenshot:

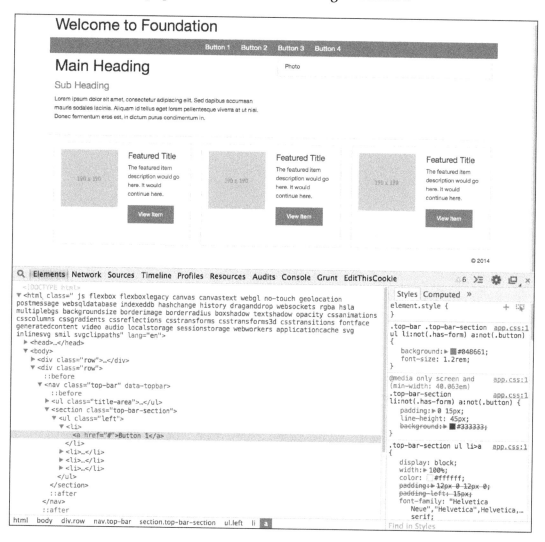

You can see from the preceding screenshot that I right-clicked on **Button 1**. You know this because that line is highlighted in the left-hand side panel in the screenshot. On the right-hand side panel, you will see the following code:

```
.top-bar .top-bar-section ul li:not(.has-form) a:not(.button) {
  background: #048661;
  font-size: 1.2rem;
}
```

You will notice that it looks quite different from what we wrote earlier; here is just the `li` item from the previous code:

```
li {

    &:not(.has-form) a:not(.button) {
       background: $primary-color;
       font-size: 1.2rem;
    }

    &:not(.has-form) a:not(.button):hover {
       background: #000;
    }
  }
```

So, how do we turn what we are getting from the Chrome inspector into Sass that can override Foundation's default settings? We first target the first element, `.top-bar .top-bar-section ul li:not(.has-form) a:not(.button)`, that is, `.top-bar`. So, let's start with this:

```
.top-bar {
  background: $primary-color;
}
```

We set `.top-bar` to have a background, and we give it the `$primary-color` Sass variable. This variable, if you remember, was set in the `settings.scss` file. If you go back to your browser, right-click on the top bar and then click on **Inspect Element**. You will see that you will get the following code in the right-hand side panel of the inspector:

```
.top-bar {
  background: #048661;
}
```

Here is a screenshot of this, so you can see where this code is coming from:

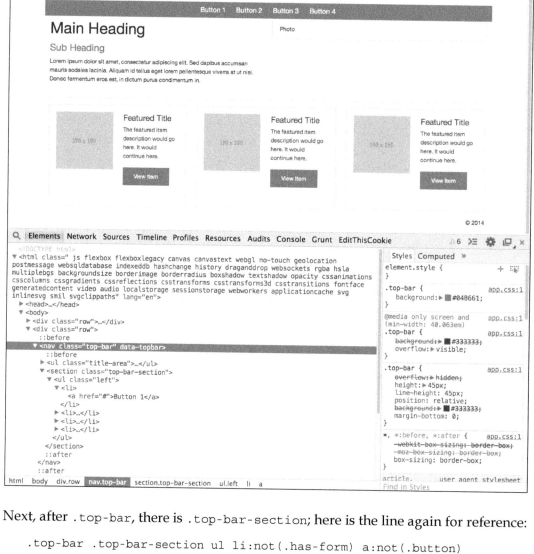

Next, after `.top-bar`, there is `.top-bar-section`; here is the line again for reference:

```
.top-bar .top-bar-section ul li:not(.has-form) a:not(.button)
```

So, we added `.top-bar-section` after `background`, as shown in the following code:

```
.top-bar {
  background: $primary-color;

  .top-bar-section {
```

```
    display: table;
    margin: auto;
  }

}
```

You will see that this is also where we put `display: table;` and `margin: auto;`. As we covered in *Chapter 7, Sass and Foundation*, we are nesting `.top-bar-section` inside `.top-bar`. This is done so that when Grunt compiles Sass, it will have `.top-bar-section` inside of `.top-bar`.

Great! Now that we have this, we target `ul` inside `.top-bar-section`, as shown in the following code:

```
.top-bar {
  background: $primary-color;

  .top-bar-section {
    display: table;
    margin: auto;

    ul {
      display: table-cell;
    }
  }

}
```

On `ul`, we have the attributes of `display: table-cell`. Now, we take a look at the next item, and it is `li:not(.has-form) a:not(.button)`; see the following line:

```
.top-bar .top-bar-section ul li:not(.has-form) a:not(.button)
```

You will notice in the following code that we broke apart `li` and `:not(.has-form) a:not(.button)`. This technically does not matter but is recommended because you might want to add some styling to all the list items that are inside `.top-bar-section` at some point. You will see that we did not add anything to the list items, but inside the list items, we have `&:not(.has-form) a:not(.button)` and `&:not(.has-form) a:not(.button):hover`. The `&:` sign tells Sass that you don't want it to put a space between `li` and `:not`. We know that there should not be a space there, because the code we got from the Chrome inspector did not have a space. It looked like this:

```
li:not(.has-form) a:not(.button)
```

Then, we gave these buttons the `background: $primary-color` and `font-size: 1.2rem;` properties, and then, we duplicated the same button line and added `:hover`. This sets what happens when the user hovers over the button. You will see that we can make the background go black with the `background: #000` code. Here is the entire code for reference:

```
.top-bar {
  background: $primary-color;

  .top-bar-section {
    display: table;
    margin: auto;

    ul {
      display: table-cell;

      li {

        &:not(.has-form) a:not(.button) {
          background: $primary-color;
          font-size: 1.2rem;
        }

        &:not(.has-form) a:not(.button):hover {
          background: #000;
        }
      }
    }

  }
}
```

You can see how we can combine Sass variables and regular old CSS together to get some pretty cool customizations. You can also see how nesting tags can really save you time from having to code everything by repeating everything. Here is how you would have had to write what we just did without Sass:

```
.top-bar {
  background: #048661;
}
.top-bar .top-bar-section {
  display: table;
  margin: auto;
}

.top-bar .top-bar-section ul {
  display: table-cell;
}

.top-bar .top-bar-section ul li:not(.has-form) a:not(.button) {
  background: #048661;
  font-size: 1.2rem;
}

.top-bar .top-bar-section ul li:not(.has-form) a:not(.button):hover {
  background: #000000;
}
```

Compare the CSS way with how you can use nesting in Sass, and you can see how much of a time saver using Sass can be.

In the previous code, you might be wondering how we got the button's hover state. If you did not know, in the **Styles** tab in the far right of the Chrome inspector, you will see a plus sign and a mouse cursor with a dashed border around it. If you click on this, you can get other CSS states by checking the boxes of the states that you want to see. This is super useful and will really help you find which CSS is applied to that element.

You can see that we have the :hover states selected, and you can see in the following code that we have the black background applied to the :hover state:

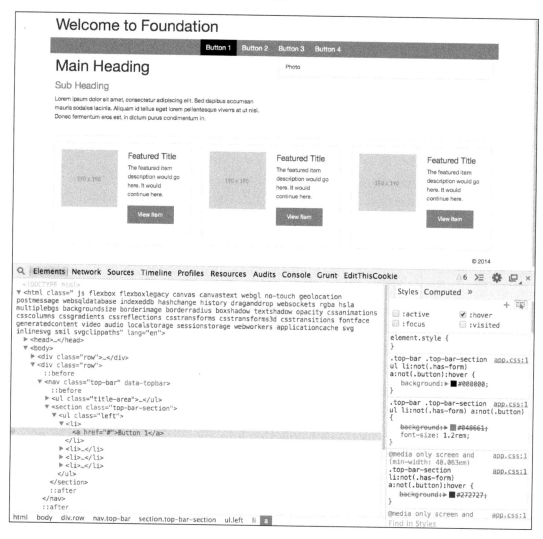

Now, let's give some love to a few more elements. Let's give some margin to the `h1` element. So, in your `_theme.scs` file on line 1, let's add:

```
h1 {
  margin-top: 3rem;
}
```

Now, on line 32, let's add:

```
.panel {
  margin-top: 3rem;
}
```

You will see that the panel moves down and is not right up against our navigation bar. Here is a screenshot of these changes:

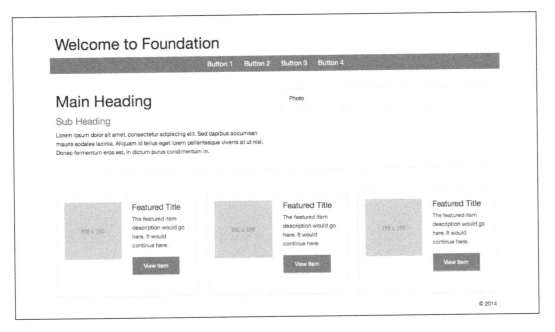

Great! We have nice-looking home page with some color and some padding, and we can keep going, but let's talk about mobile. If you resize the browser down to a small screen, you will get something like what's shown in the following screenshot:

You will likely want to change some of the padding on a mobile or small screen, so let's try some of this right now by adding some media queries. So, let's add a media query inside of .panel inside of our _theme.scss file on or around line 35, and it will look like this:

```scss
.panel {
  margin-top: 3rem;

  @media only screen and (max-width: 40em) {
    margin-top: auto;
  }
}
```

You will see that we are setting margin-top back to auto when the screen has a max-width value equal to 40em. If you refresh your browser, you will notice that the margin is gone when your browser is small or you are on a small-screen device, such as a phone.

Here is the screenshot:

This works but is not the best way to do this, especially when you are setting and then unsetting something. For a mobile-first and responsive approach, what makes more sense is to only set `margin-top` when the screen is big enough to have this margin; so, let's change our `.panel` code to the following:

```
.panel {
  @media only screen and (min-width: 40.063em) {
    margin-top: 3rem;
  }
}
```

You will notice that we changed the media query from `max-width` to `min-width`, and we moved `margin-top: 3rem;` inside the media query and got rid of everything else. Not only can you write less code, but you are also not overriding your own code; you are just adding your customizations as the screen size gets bigger.

For a list of all the Foundation media queries, you can visit `http://foundation.zurb.com/docs/media-queries.html`.

Now, you might have noticed a few other things that need fixing when you have been resizing the browser. For one, the featured title is pretty close to our images on a small screen, as you can see in the following screenshot:

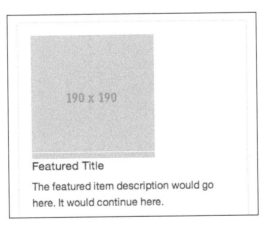

Let's fix this. As we only want this to be fixed on a small screen, let's use the `max-width` media query. So, on or around line 38 in the `_theme.scss` file, let's add the following:

```
@media only screen and (max-width: 40em) {
    h4 {
      margin-top: 1rem;
    }
  }
```

The complete code will look like this:

```
.panel {

  @media only screen and (min-width: 40.063em) {
    margin-top: 3rem;
  }

  @media only screen and (max-width: 40em) {
    h4 {
      margin-top: 1rem;
    }
  }
}
```

Go ahead and refresh your browser. You will see that we now have a margin on h4 (**Feature Title**), as shown in the following screenshot:

Nice! This is starting to take shape, but you might have noticed that the formatting of **Featured Title** goes way when we are on a medium-sized screen or when we have resized our browser between a small and large screen size, as shown in the following screenshot:

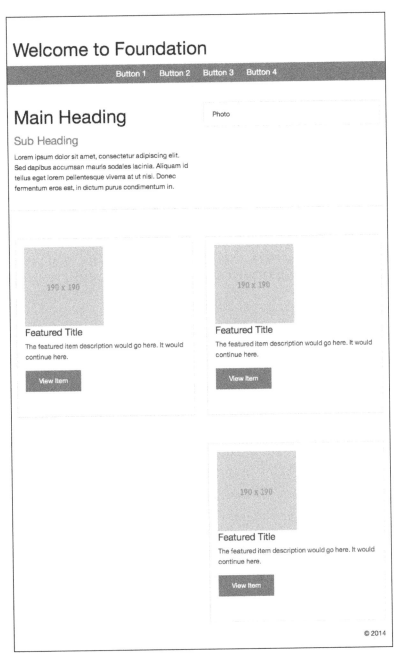

So, let's fix this by changing `max-width` to include the max width of the medium screen as well. As we did not change the default grid ranges set by Foundation, we can use the `min-width` and `max-width` settings right from the Foundation documentation found at `http://foundation.zurb.com/docs/media-queries.html`. You will see that the medium grid size's `max-width` is `64em`. This is what we changed: `40em` to `64em`. Here is the code:

```
.panel {

    @media only screen and (min-width: 40.063em) {
      margin-top: 3rem;
    }

    @media only screen and (max-width: 64em) {
      h4 {
        margin-top: 1rem;
      }
    }
}
```

Go ahead and refresh your browser. You will see that we now have the same margin in the medium-sized screens, as shown in the following screenshot:

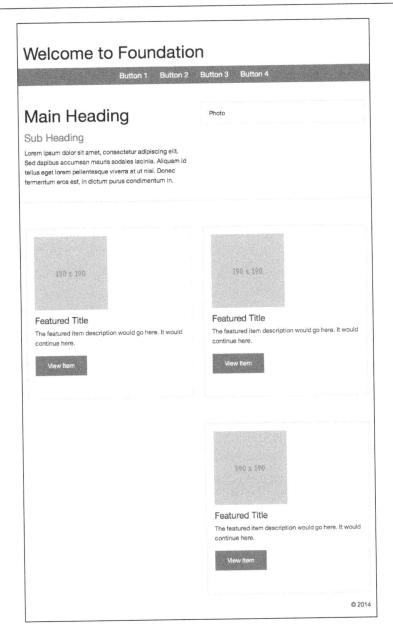

Things are starting to look pretty good at all three grid ranges—small, medium, and large—but I am sure you have noticed by now that the third featured item is aligned to the right on a medium screen, and there is a white space to the left of it. You might like this now, but let's fix this just on the medium-sized screen. So, we need to figure out what is causing the last featured item to align to the right.

By default, Foundation aligns the last item in the grid to the right. However, you will not always know what is causing something you want to change, so let's use the Chrome **Web Inspector** to figure it out. Here is a screenshot of what we want to change, and then, let's cover how to get there:

You will see that we have `<div class="small-12 medium-6 large-4 columns">` selected, and if you have any experience with the Chrome **Web Inspector**, you will know that when you right-click on an element and hit **Inspect**, you do not always get the right element you want. Getting `<div class="small-12 medium-6 large-4 columns">` selected is the perfect example of this. What is more likely to happen is that you are going to right-click on the element and hit **Inspect**, and you will get the wrong element. This is OK and normal, so when you try and inspect the panel that is aligned to the right in our case, you will likely get one of the large six-column divs below the line we have highlighted in the previous screenshot. This at least gets you in the area of the code you need to modify to get the third panel to align to the left. So, what we do is move up line by line by clicking on the lines. We can hover over the different CSS tags in the right-hand side panel of the inspector and change or turn off the values until we find what is causing our issue. Once we find the issue, we can write some CSS code in our `_theme.scss` file to fix our problem.

If you go back to the screenshot, you will see that we have `<div class="small-12 medium-6 large-4 columns">` selected, and if you look at the right-hand side panel, you will see the following:

```
@media only screen and (min-width: 40.063em)
[class*="column"]+[class*="column"]:last-child {
  float: right;
}
```

As you can see, Foundation is setting `last-child` to `float: right`. You will also notice that it is in a media query, starting at the medium screen range. How do we know the medium screen range? This is found on the media query link from the Foundation documentation at `http://foundation.zurb.com/docs/media-queries.html`.

So, let's go ahead and add this to our code on or around line 32. As shown in the following code, make sure it is before `.panel` in `_theme.scss` and after the closing braces (}) of `top-bar`:

```
@media only screen and (min-width: 40.063em) {
    [class*="column"]+[class*="column"]:last-child {
      float: left;
    }
}
```

Also, note that the code you get from the inspector with media queries will not work properly with Sass. You need to make sure that you add a starting brace ({) after `min-width: 40.063em` and a second one (}) at the end of the media query.

Refresh your browser. You will see that it works: the third featured item is aligned to the left, as shown in the following screenshot:

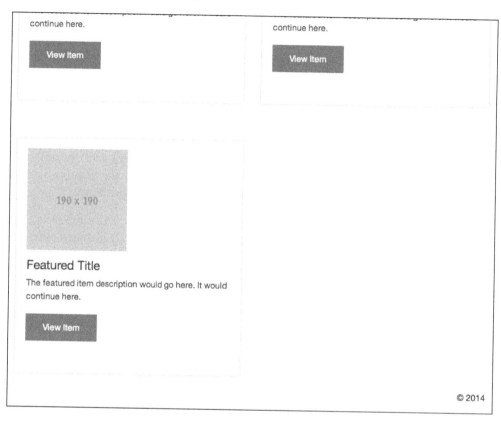

The way we fixed this, however, is not correct. We modified every :last-child element with min-width: 40.063em. So, let's fix this. This is a pretty simple fix. Let's just wrap our media query in .featured. If you remember, earlier, we added a .featured class to the row that contains the featured items. Here is the code:

```
.featured {
  @media only screen and (min-width: 40.063em) {
    [class*="column"]+[class*="column"]:last-child {
      float: left;
    }
  }
}
```

We could take this a step further and move the `.panel` code inside the `.featured` class and after the media query, because right now, we are modifying every panel on the page. This is fine for our example, but if we added another row with panels, they will get the same formatting as our featured items' panels.

As you can see, for in-browser design, all you need to do is start laying out your page just like we did and keep changing and adding CSS to theme your design right in the browser. You need to constantly see how your changes affect the other two grid sizes, and you need to make sure that you only make changes in the grid range in which you want to make the changes. If you want changes in multiple grid sizes, you need to use `min-width` and `max-width` to handle this. You also need to add styles only to the grid sizes in which you need these changes; this is better than trying to override your own Sass, as the screen size changes.

Foundation theme

Now, you might not have the time or you do not feel comfortable with designing, so you can use a UI theme. There are a few floating around online, but here is the most popular one:

`http://websymphony.net/almost-flat-ui/`

If you want to use this theme, instead of downloading Foundation from the Zurb website, download it from the previous link. This theme is using the Sass version of Foundation, so you might need to follow the setup at `http://foundation.zurb.com/docs/sass.html`.

If you want to see what others have done with Foundation, you can always visit the Zurb responsive gallery at `http://zurb.com/responsive`.

Creating Foundation grids in Photoshop

You might not be fully comfortable designing in the browser, so there are a few places online that have created Foundation grids for you:

- `http://www.thebandagency.ca/design-templates-for-foundation-framework/` has Illustrator and Photoshop grid files
- `http://www.yeedeen.com/downloads/category/30-psd` has Photoshop files

If you want to use a custom grid size and design in Photoshop, Illustrator, GIMP, or Inkscape, there is a great online tool at `http://www.gridlover.net/foundation/`. What you do is adjust the grid's `max-width` slider, set your gutter and the column number, and then you can take a screenshot of the grid and open this file in any of the programs listed earlier. You can then use guides in that program to mark out the grid based on the screenshot. You can do this for multiple sizes based on your media queries, so you can design for small, medium, and large grid sizes.

Using these grids in Photoshop will help you really speed up the design process and make converting your designs into Foundation a lot faster. It also really helps the person who is coding your designs.

Summary

In this chapter, we covered how to customize theme Foundation components, and then we moved on to talk about some UI themes and how to use or create grids for use in Photoshop.

In the next chapter, we will see how to use Foundation with a content-management system.

10
Foundation with Other Tools

We have covered a lot in this book, but we have not really covered how to use Foundation with a content management system or how you can use it with a programming language.

We will be covering the following topics in this chapter:

- Finding a starter theme
- Using Foundation with multiple programming languages
- Ideas on how to play nice with developers

Finding a starter theme

Foundation can and has been used with pretty much any content management system, and the Foundation community has been great in creating paid and free starter themes for your use. For those of you who are not familiar with a starter theme, this is a base theme that is created for a content management system or programming language; it takes Foundation and creates a starter theme for WordPress, Drupal, and Joomla, which you can start with to create your project from. This is similar to what Zurb gives you with Foundation when you first download it and open the index.html file.

You see a bunch of the Foundation components inside the grid, as shown in the following screenshot:

Zurb has a great list of these starter themes at `http://foundation.zurb.com/develop/tools.html`. The following screenshot shows the list of the starter themes that you will find on the site:

Wordpress

JointsWP by Jeremy Englert using F5
WP-Forge by Thomas E. Vasquez using F5
FoundationPress by Ole Fredrik Lie using F5
Picotto by Jonathan Urban using F5 (New!)
Spine by Paul de Wouters using F5
NARGA by Nguyễn Đình Quân using F5
Corner Stone by Stephen Mullen using F5
Reverie by Zhen using F5
WPBaseFoundation by Steven Loyer using F5
Rootbeer by Josh Medeski using F5 (New!)
Clean Yeti by Serene Themes using F5 (New!)
Green Yeti by Serene Themes using F5 (New!)
Basey by Zach Schnackel using F5
Starter Theme by Drew Morris using F4 (New!)
Reactor by Anthony Wilhelm using F4
f415 by Gabor Javorszky using F4
required+ Themes by required+ using F3.25
Yeti by Modular Learning using F3.2 (New!)
WP-Foundation by 320press using F3
Yotta by Dieter using F3 (New!)

Joomla

JoomberUI by The Template Blog (New!)
Joomla Template by Arnold Mwumva Ford, Meridian Softech
Joomla Template by Antony Doyle, Siege21

Drupal

Drupal Theme by Drew Kennelly
Zurb Foundation Supporting F3.2, F4 & Drupal 8 by Chris Lee,

Foundation CSS Themes

Base 2013 by Dieter using F3 (New!)
RGB by Dieter using F3 (New!)
PhotoBiz by Dieter using F3 (New!)
Ultraslim by Dieter using F3 (New!)
Epic Using F3 (New!)

Python

Pyramid Scaffold by Parker Pinette

CodeIgniter

Responsive CodeIgniter BoilerPlate by Arnold Mwumva Ford, Meridian Softech using Foundation 3

Shopify

Foundationify Shopify Theme by Luke Bussey using Foundation 5
Shopify Foundation Theme Framework by Cam Gould using Foundation 5 (New!)

SilverStripe

Foundation Silverstripe Theme by Ryan Wachtl using Foundation 5

Orchard

Foundation Theme for Orchard CMS using Foundation 4

They update this list on a regular basis and you should check it often. You will notice that most of today's popular languages have a theme that is listed on the Zurb tools site.

FoundationPress (https://github.com/olefredrik/foundationpress/) is a popular WordPress theme that has a nice-looking demo site, as shown in the following screenshot:

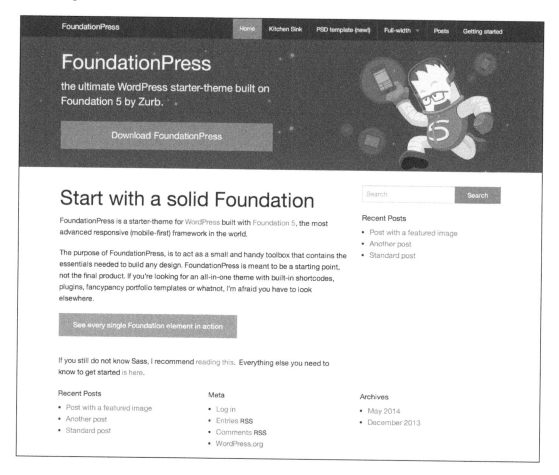

Here is a great example of a Foundation 4 theme; it is a Magento-based theme that I purchased and used on a project:

http://addonbakery.com/magento-themes/magento-polarcore-theme

Here is a screenshot of the template:

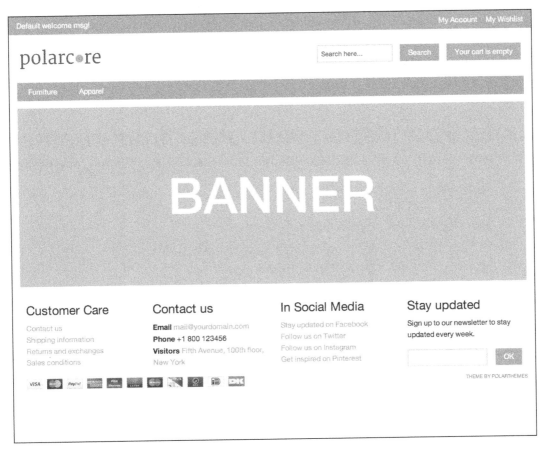

You will realize that spending money on a theme can save you a lot of time when you think about how long it would take you to roll your own Magento, WordPress, Drupal, or whichever language you are looking to use. Personally, before Foundation was released to the public, I built my own responsive theme, and it worked. However, I was not able to build a better responsive theme than a community- or company-backed responsive framework such as Foundation. So, I decided to move my projects to Foundation and have never looked back. Once you get comfortable with Foundation and are constantly using it with say, Drupal, you might want to create a base theme that you can start with and only use what your projects need on a regular basis. The other great thing about using a popular framework such as Foundation is that people create snippets for your favorite code editors such as `https://github.com/zurb/foundation-5-sublime-snippets` for Sublime Text.

If you do not know what snippets are, they are blocks of code that are commonly used over and over again, so instead of typing them over and over again, you can use a snippet and modify it, if needed, after you add it to your code. A snippet would be similar to a mixin, which we talked about in *Chapter 8, Mixins*.

Another great place to look for templates, code, and resources is Zurb's playground at `http://zurb.com/playground`.

Using Foundation with other frameworks

The following is a list of links that shows Foundation used with different frameworks:

- Foundation with Rails can be found at
  `http://foundation.zurb.com/docs/applications.html`
- Foundation with Angular can be found at
  `http://madmimi.github.io/angular-foundation/`
- Foundation with Python can be found at
  `https://pypi.python.org/pypi/pinax-theme-foundation`
- Foundation with .NET can be found at
  `http://www.responsivemvc.net/Foundation`
- Foundation with Meteor can be found at
  `https://atmospherejs.com/package/zurb-foundation`

As you can see from the preceding list, there are many languages you can use Foundation with. If you visit `http://foundation.zurb.com/develop/tools.html`, you will see that Zurb is constantly updating Foundation with other resources, languages, and frameworks that support Foundation. I also encourage you to start your own Foundation GitHub repository for the community and yourself to contribute to.

Ideas on how to play nice with developers

As a designer and/or a frontend developer, you should try to understand as much as possible about every team member's job. In my opinion, the more you understand how each person views their part of the project, the better designer/frontend developer you will be. Nowadays, things are very complicated and there are many layers of technologies stacked on top of each other to build even the simplest of web projects. The thing is, everyone thinks that their part of the project is the most important and that their part should have the most time and/or budget spent on it. However, from my personal experience, I can say that you really need to learn and understand the job roles of other members of your team.

As a designer, you think that fonts, font size, line heights, and a little more or less padding will make or break a project, but is it worth spending hours getting all those things just perfect? On some projects, of course, it is; on others, it is the last thing the project needs. The trick with any role in this industry, especially that of a designer, is understanding as much as possible about how the design will be built. In Photoshop, or whatever you use, you can create anything. In my opinion, you need to be thinking about how what you design will be coded. If you do not know whether something can be built, you should ask your developer. I can't stress how important communicating with your team can be.

With responsive design how, is what gets designed going to work on a desktop, tablet, and phone? What happens when the screen size is neither equal to the size of a phone nor of a tablet? The more you understand about how the project will be built, the better your project will be in the end. This is why I really believe in moving away from Photoshop and doing responsive prototyping right at the beginning of the project, like we covered at the beginning of this book.

These design, frontend, and development issues can be sorted out for the most part before the client sees anything. Also, if you are using this approach for a web app, you can user test new ideas faster and with little effort. The most aggravating thing for developers is not being able to build what gets designed and signed off by the client, and all this happens before they even see the design of the project. If you are a designer, try and learn a little bit of programming, not so you can become a programmer but so that you can understand where programmers are coming from and where their struggling points can come from. If you are a developer, try and learn the basics of designing so that you can see where a designer is coming from. Being able to relate to all your team members is super important.

Let me give you a few of examples: let's say you are building a simple WordPress brochure website with five pages. As a designer, you can pretty much do whatever you like. You show a developer, get their approval, and for the most part, there should not be a lot of major changes to the site's structure. However, if you are building a responsive site, you should be thinking about the design and content flow and how the layout will be on the different screen sizes. These types of sites can have their challenges, but the challenges can be sorted out in a few quick meetings.

Now let's say you have a Drupal site that has hundreds of pages, needs to be very user friendly, must be available in multiple languages, needs a search option, and should be responsive. This is a challenging project. There will be pain points for the user on certain parts of the project or certain parts based on device that unless you have a budget to perform user testing and iteration will likely have to be left and just dealt with. This can be a hard pill to swallow for certain parts of the team, but these are the trade-offs you need to make due to factors such as budget and timeline.

Now, let's say you are building a startup and you have chosen Ruby on Rails. You get a basic Rails install set up and running on your computer. You get Foundation installed and are ready to start making your company a reality. You of course, want the best user experience, the sexiest design, the perfect number of features, and billions of users. This is a daunting task and you will need to make a lot of trade-offs to get to all of these, and to be honest, you will never be 100 percent happy with every aspect of the project. So, let's say you have one month to build version 1 of your app; you will need to cut corners, leave features out, and release something that is rough around the edges. That line height on those homepage callouts is not that important anymore on a tight deadline like this. Also, consider that you design something killer, even an award winner, but the development team only has time to implement half, or even worse, one quarter of your ideas. This will affect the design and user experience in a huge way, but sometimes having something is better than nothing, even if it is rough.

I truly believe that everyone at a company should be trying to improve the user experience of the project or product, but what is important to different departments can really change how things need to work. For example, what is important to the sales team, from a user-experience side might be totally different from that of a regular user.

How do you handle the interface, does it change, does it have a built-in walk through of features, if there is a walkthrough, do you show it once or a few times? How does this walkthrough work on a touch device, do we even show it on a touch or phone screen? All of these design and frontend decisions have a huge impact on the user experience, but how much time does the development team have to help you implement them?

Once you have something you really think is great, you should user test it. What if all the users you test on hate it, do not get it, or you realize the user uses that section in a way you never considered? Do you redo that whole section or only a part of it? If you decide to redo only a part of it, which part will it be? Is there time to implement all, some, or a part of these changes?

These three examples are just the tip of the iceberg of the challenges you will face as the projects and apps get more complicated in your web career. So, compromise and try and understand what you can do in the time and budget allotted. This will make your projects go a lot smoother, and you will be able to talk about the problems/solutions you came up with based on time and budget when you are looking for other work. This experience and open mindedness will make you a huge asset to any team.

Summary

In this chapter, we covered how to get up and running with some starter themes for an array of languages. We also covered how to use Foundation with a bunch of programming languages, as well as my experience working in a team of people and trying to understand where other people on the team are coming from.

Where to go from here

Like anything in life, it takes practice, but do not give up. Reach out and get involved in the online and offline community in your area. People are willing to help and love to talk about what they are passionate about. Keep learning and chase your passions in this industry. There will be ups and downs, but just remember how lucky we all are to be working in such a changing and evolving industry. Feel free to reach out to me; I would love to hear from you and what you build with Foundation. Thanks for reading.

Index

Symbols

<a> tag 52
.bowerrc file 134
.gitignore file 134
<h1> tag 48
<kbd> tag 65
<li> tag 50
<nav> element 31
<nav> tag 39
.scss file
  converting, to app.scss file 132
<section> element 31
_settings.scss file 121-123
<ul> tag 53

A

accordion 97-99
Adobe Edge Inspect
  URL 108
alerts 68
app.scss file
  about 130
  converting, to .scss file 132

B

base theme
  overview 10-12
block grid 23
blockquote 51
Bourbon
  about 144
  URL 144

Bower

Bower
  about 119, 131
  URL 131
bower.json file 134
breadcrumbs
  creating 38, 39
BrowserStack
  about 111
  URL 111
buttons
  about 52
  button groups, creating 55-57
  drop-down buttons 53
  split drop-down buttons 55

C

Chrome simulation 108-110
clearing 90, 91
Codio
  about 133
  URL 117
columns, grid
  centering 21, 22
custom grid
  URL 8

D

definition lists 51
designer/frontend developers
  relationships, maintaining 184-186
drop-down buttons
  about 53
  with images and text 54

E

element position, grid
  setting, based on screen size 25, 26
elements
  about 47
  blockquote 51
  buttons 52
  keystrokes 65
  label 65
  lists 49
  panels 57-60
  pricing tables 60
  progress bars 64, 65
  tables 63, 64
  typography 48
  v-cards 52
  video 64

F

forms 91-93
form validation 94
Foundation
  elements 47
  framework 9, 10
  grid 17, 18
  IE6, testing 107
  IE7, testing 107
  JavaScript components 75
  mixins, using within 139-143
  navigation 31
  pagination 39
  unsupported versions of IE, supporting 106
  URL, for migration guide 13
  used, for designing in-browser 145-147
  using, with other frameworks 184
  version migration 13
Foundation component
  URL, for documentation 144
foundation.css file 11
Foundation documentation
  referring to 13
  URL 13
Foundation media queries
  URL 169
foundation.min.css file 11
foundation.min.js file 12

FoundationPress
  URL 182
Foundation prototypes 7
Foundation, versions
  about 9
  complete 9
  custom 9
  essentials 9
  reference link 9
  SCSS 9
Foundation with Angular
  URL 184
Foundation with Meteor
  URL 184
Foundation with .NET
  URL 184
Foundation with Python
  URL 184
Foundation with Rails
  URL 184
Foundation with Sass
  installing 116-121

G

Ghostlab
  about 108
  URL 108
Git
  URL 7, 14, 117
grid
  block grid 23
  columns, centering 21, 22
  creating, in Photoshop 177, 178
  element position, setting based on
    screen size 25, 26
  nesting 24
  offsetting 22
  online resources 177
  overview 19-21
grid sizes 18
Grid templating tool
  about 21
  URL 21
Grunt
  about 119, 132
  URL 120, 132

Gruntfile.js file 134
guest additions, virtual machine
  installing 106

H

hr tags 51
humans.txt file 134

I

icon bar 72, 73
IE6
  testing, for Foundation 107
IE 6-11 versions
  testing 101-106
IE7
  testing, for Foundation 107
in-browser
  designing, Foundation used 145-147
index.html file 10, 131, 134
inline lists 50
installation, Foundation with Sass
  about 116-121
  complications 133
  requisites 116
interchange responsive background
        images 87
interchange responsive content
  about 83-86
  interchange responsive background
        images 87
  interchange responsive default content 86
  interchange responsive images 86
  retina media queries 87
interchange responsive default content 86
interchange responsive images
  about 86
  with media queries 87

J

JavaScript components
  about 75
  accordion 97-99
  clearing 90, 91
  forms 91-93

form validation 94
Joyride 96
Magellan Sticky Nav 77-80
off-canvas navigation 80-83
Orbit slider 88-90
Reveal 95
tabs 99
Joyride 96
jquery.js file 12
JS files
  reviewing 133

K

Keynote
  about 111
  URL 111
keystrokes 65

L

label
  about 65
  alerts 68
  icon bar 72, 73
  print styles 65
  sliders 65-67
  switches 72
  tooltips 68, 69
  utility classes 69
  visibility classes 70, 71
Libsass
  URL 120
lists
  about 49
  definition lists 51
  inline lists 50
lorem ipsum
  URL 78

M

Magellan sticky navigation
        (Magellan Sticky Nav)
  about 77-80
  code explanation 80
Magento-based theme
  URL 182

mixin libraries
  about 144
  Bourbon 144
mixins
  about 135-138
  Sass CSS3 mixins 144
  Sass mixins 144
  Sassy buttons 144
  URL 141
  using, within Foundation 139-143
  using, within Sass 139-143
Modernizr
  URL 8
modernizr.js file 12
multiple device testing
  about 107, 108
  Chrome simulation 108-110
  remote debugging 108

N

navigation
  about 31
  breadcrumbs, creating 38, 39
  reference link 36
  side navigation, creating 38
  subnavigation, creating 38
navigation bar
  about 31-36
  tweaking 36, 37
nesting, grid 24
NodeJS
  URL 117
node_modules folder 133
normalize.css file 11

O

off-canvas navigation 80-83
offsetting, grid 22
one-page demo website
  advanced navigation, creating 40-44
  building 26-29
  overview 15
  theme, modifying 26-29

Online Android Emulator
  about 111
  URL 111
Orbit slider 88-90

P

package.json file 134
pagination 39
panels 57-60
Photoshop
  grid, creating in 177, 178
Photoshop grid templates
  URL 8
pricing tables
  about 60
  border issues, fixing 62
  creating, in columns 61
  creating, in columns without gutter 61
print styles 65
progress bars 64, 65
projects
  prototyping 8
prototype
  about 6
  building 148-152
  customizing 155-177
  reviewing 153-155
prototyping 6-8

R

README.md file 134
remote debugging 108
Responsive Inspector
  about 111
  URL 111
responsive tables
  URL 64
retina media queries 87
Reveal 95
robots.txt file 134
Ruby 1.9+
  URL 117

S

Sass
  about 114-116
  mixins, using within 139-143
  URL 113
  URL, for installation 113, 132
  variables 123-130
Sass CSS3 mixins
  URL 144
Sass mixins
  URL 144
Sassy buttons
  about 144
  URL 144
Sauce Labs
  about 111
  URL 111
side navigation
  creating 38
sliders 65-67
small tag 49
source ordering 25
split drop-down buttons 55
starter theme
  about 179
  searching 179-184
  URL 181
sticky navigation 77
subheadings 48
Sublime Text snippets
  URL 183
subnavigation
  creating 38
Subversion
  URL 7
switches 72

T

tables 63, 64
tabs 99
theme
  modifying, for one-page
    demo website 26-29
  online resources 177
  using 177

tools, used for testing
  BrowserStack 111
  Keynote 111
  Online Android Emulator 111
  Responsive Inspector 111
  Sauce Labs 111
tooltips 68, 69
typography
  about 48
  small tag 49
  subheadings 48

U

utility classes
  about 69
  hide class 69
  left class 69
  right class 69
  text-center class 69
  text-justify class 69
  text-left class 69
  text-right class 69
  URL 69

V

variables 123-130
v-cards
  about 52
  reference link 52
version migration, Foundation
  browser support 14
  framework support 14
video 64
VirtualBox
  URL 102
virtual machine
  guest additions, installing 106
  installing 104
  URL, for downloading 101
visibility classes
  about 70, 71
  hidden-for-large-only class 71
  hidden-for-large-up class 71
  hidden-for-medium-only class 71
  hidden-for-medium-up class 71

hidden-for-small-only class 71
hidden-for-xlarge-only class 71
hidden-for-xlarge-up class 71
hidden-for-xxlarge-up class 71
hide-for-large-only class 70
hide-for-large-up class 70
hide-for-medium-only class 70
hide-for-medium-up class 70
hide-for-touch class 70
hide-for-xlarge-only class 70
hide-for-xlarge-up class 70
hide-for-xxlarge-up class 70
show-for-large-only class 70
show-for-large-up class 70
show-for-medium-only class 70
show-for-medium-up class 70
show-for-small-only class 70
show-for-touch class 70
show-for-xlarge-only class 70
show-for-xlarge-up class 70
show-for-xxlarge-up class 70
visible-for-large-only class 71
visible-for-large-up class 71
visible-for-medium-only class 71
visible-for-medium-up class 71
visible-for-small-only class 71
visible-for-xlarge-only class 71
visible-for-xlarge-up class 71
visible-for-xxlarge-up class 71

W

wireframing 6

Z

Zurb
  about 13
  Foundation, extending 15
  URL, for browser and device compatibility
    list 14
  URL, for change log 13
  URL, for support 14
Zurb responsive gallery
  URL 177
Zurb's playground
  URL 15, 184

Thank you for buying
Learning Zurb Foundation

About Packt Publishing

Packt, pronounced 'packed', published its first book *"Mastering phpMyAdmin for Effective MySQL Management"* in April 2004 and subsequently continued to specialize in publishing highly focused books on specific technologies and solutions.

Our books and publications share the experiences of your fellow IT professionals in adapting and customizing today's systems, applications, and frameworks. Our solution based books give you the knowledge and power to customize the software and technologies you're using to get the job done. Packt books are more specific and less general than the IT books you have seen in the past. Our unique business model allows us to bring you more focused information, giving you more of what you need to know, and less of what you don't.

Packt is a modern, yet unique publishing company, which focuses on producing quality, cutting-edge books for communities of developers, administrators, and newbies alike. For more information, please visit our website: www.packtpub.com.

About Packt Open Source

In 2010, Packt launched two new brands, Packt Open Source and Packt Enterprise, in order to continue its focus on specialization. This book is part of the Packt Open Source brand, home to books published on software built around Open Source licenses, and offering information to anybody from advanced developers to budding web designers. The Open Source brand also runs Packt's Open Source Royalty Scheme, by which Packt gives a royalty to each Open Source project about whose software a book is sold.

Writing for Packt

We welcome all inquiries from people who are interested in authoring. Book proposals should be sent to author@packtpub.com. If your book idea is still at an early stage and you would like to discuss it first before writing a formal book proposal, contact us; one of our commissioning editors will get in touch with you.

We're not just looking for published authors; if you have strong technical skills but no writing experience, our experienced editors can help you develop a writing career, or simply get some additional reward for your expertise.

Getting Started with Zurb Foundation 4

ISBN: 978-1-78216-596-5   Paperback: 126 pages

Design and build professional websites with Zurb Foundation's mobile-first responsive framework

1. Get up to speed quickly with Foundation's responsive grid system.

2. Integrate easy-to-configure CSS components into your website.

3. Add powerful JavaScript plugins to your web pages.

Instant Zurb Foundation 4

ISBN: 978-1-78216-402-9   Paperback: 56 pages

Get up and running in an instant with Zurb Foundation 4 Framework

1. Learn something new in an Instant! A short, fast, focused guide delivering immediate results.

2. Construct responsive and mobile-ready web pages without worrying about browser-related issues. Just code once and it will be compatible with all browsers and display sizes.

3. Learn to use Foundation 4 features with actual code examples and ample screenshots.

Please check **www.PacktPub.com** for information on our titles

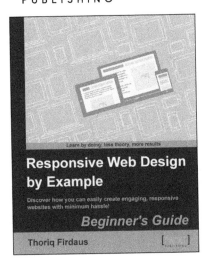

Responsive Web Design by Example Beginner's Guide

ISBN: 978-1-84969-542-8   Paperback: 338 pages

Discover how you can easily create engaging, responsive websites with minimum hassle!

1. Rapidly develop and prototype responsive websites by utilizing powerful open source frameworks.

2. Focus less on the theory and more on results, with clear step-by-step instructions, previews, and examples to help you along the way.

3. Learn how you can utilize three of the most powerful responsive frameworks available today: Bootstrap, Skeleton, and Zurb Foundation.

HTML5 and CSS3 Responsive Web Design Cookbook

ISBN: 978-1-84969-544-2   Paperback: 204 pages

Learn the secrets of developing responsive websites capable of interfacing with today's mobile Internet devices

1. Learn the fundamental elements of writing responsive website code for all stages of the development lifecycle.

2. Create the ultimate code writer's resource using logical workflow layers.

3. Full of usable code for immediate use in your website projects.

Please check **www.PacktPub.com** for information on our titles

CPSIA information can be obtained
at www.ICGtesting.com
Printed in the USA
BVHW02s0921261117
501257BV00004B/30/P